Business Models for the Social Mobile Cloud

Business Models for the Social Mobile Cloud

TRANSFORM YOUR BUSINESS USING SOCIAL MEDIA, MOBILE INTERNET, AND CLOUD COMPUTING

Ted Shelton

WILEY

John Wiley & Sons, Inc.

Cover image: © Volodymyr Grinko/iStockphoto
Cover design: John Wiley & Sons, Inc.

Published by John Wiley & Sons, Inc., Hoboken, New Jersey.
Published simultaneously in Canada.

For general information on our other products and services or for technical support, please contact our Customer Care Department within the United States at (800) 762-2974, outside the United States at (317) 572-3993 or fax (317) 572-4002.

Wiley publishes in a variety of print and electronic formats and by print-on-demand. Some material included with standard print versions of this book may not be included in e-books or in print-on-demand. If this book refers to media such as a CD or DVD that is not included in the version you purchased, you may download this material at http://booksupport.wiley.com. For more information about Wiley products, visit www.wiley.com.

Library of Congress Cataloging-in-Publication Data:

Shelton, Ted, 1966–
   Business models for the social mobile cloud: transform your business using social media, mobile Internet, and cloud computing / Ted Shelton.
        p. cm.
   Includes index.
   ISBN 978-1-118-36994-4 (cloth); ISBN 978-1-118-49419-6 (ebk.);
ISBN 978-1-118-49420-2 (ebk.); ISBN 978-1-118-49421-9 (ebk.);
ISBN 978-1-118-55591-0 (ebk.)
   1.   Information technology—Management. 2.   Internet marketing. 3.   Social media. 4.   Cloud computing. I. Title.
   HD30.2.S5373 2013
   658.8'72—dc23

                                                                                                 2012037682

Printed in the United States of America
10 9 8 7 6 5 4 3 2 1

To the small village of outstanding individuals who have made the creation and publication of this book possible. Without the encouragement and support of my family, the regular comments and suggestions from friends, and the belief in this project expressed by my colleagues at PwC, this book would still be another unfinished project. Thank you to all of you!

Contents

Preface: There's an App for That!   xi

Introduction: Turning Inside Out   1

PART I   THE TECHNOLOGY OF THE SOCIAL MOBILE CLOUD   5

Chapter 1   **A Remote Control for the World**   7
             The Three Technologies   7
             Lessons from the History of the Internet   9
             The History Lesson: Big Picture Thinkers Survive the Game   12
             Build for the Social Mobile Cloud   15
             The Time Is *Now*   16
             Social Networking Is the Fastest Growing Technology Ever   17
             The Cloud: The Connective Tissue   18
             Buy a Smartphone Now   20

Chapter 2   **Social Means Connected: Compete with Yourself,
             Collaborate with Others**   23
             The Social Network   24
             Co-Creation   28
             Compete with Yourself   29
             Sign Up for a Social Network Today—on Your New Smartphone   30
             Your Employees and Business Partners in Social Networks   32

Chapter 3   **Mobile: The Great Untethering**   35
             The New Technical Capabilities   36
             Connectivity   38

Reality Redefined: The Physical World with Data Overlay   40

Life Streaming: Access to a Photographic Memory   41

Cyborg   42

BYOD and the Consumerization of IT   43

Chapter 4   **Plug Yourself into the Cloud**   45

Four Key Technologies   45

Benefits of the Cloud Are Heavenly for Business   47

Drawbacks of the Cloud—Just Like Any Grid   48

Leveling the Playing Field   49

Plug Yourself into the Cloud   50

PART II   HOW BUSINESS WILL BE CHANGED BY THE SOCIAL
              MOBILE CLOUD   51

Chapter 5   **ADAPT: Adapting to Change**   53

Technological Changes   53

At the Core of Today's Change: Transaction Cost Economics   56

Chapter 6   **Persistent Digital Engagement: The New Digital Consumer**   59

Customer Service Is the New Marketing   61

Connecting Digitally at the Physical Point of Sale   61

Embrace Transparency   63

Chapter 7   **Digitization: The Rising Value of Information in
              Products and Services**   65

Innovation Drivers   66

Wireless Sensors in Everything and Everywhere   67

Application Programming Interfaces for Everything   68

Software Is Everywhere   68

Chapter 8   **Crowd Storming, Crowd Sourcing, Collaboration, Co-Creation**   71

More People = Faster and Better Decisions   72

Group Collaboration = Faster and Better Outcomes   72

Extend Engagement and You Increase Value for Everyone   73

Chapter 9   **Hierarchy Will Yield to Networks, Remaking Organizations**   75

Seniority and Control of Information   75

Finding New Business Model Solutions   77

Chapter 10   **How We Buy: Redefining Shopping and Payment**   79
Business Model Shift 1: For Retailers, the Customer Is in Control   79
Business Model Shift 2: Pay from the Comfort of Your Own Phone   82
Business Model Shift 3: Corporate Currencies   85
Business Model Shift 4: Insuring Corporate Currencies   87
Business Model Shift 5: Accepting (Multicurrency) Mobile Payments   88
Business Model Shift 6: Transforming the Purchase Experience with
Mobile Payments   89

Chapter 11   **The Game of Work, the Work of Game**   93
Business Model Shift 7: Turning Work into a Game   93
Business Model Shift 8: Data-Driven Decision Making and a Culture of
Experimentation   97
Business Model Shift 9: Experience Is the Dominant Value   103

Chapter 12   **Work and the Workplace Reimagined**   105
Forces of Change   105
Business Model Shift 10: Dynamic Networked Social Sales and Support Staff   107
Business Model Shift 11: Workforce Collaboration to Improve Safety and Quality   110
Business Model Shift 12: Transparency and Openness   111

PART III   UNDERSTANDING CHANGE: HOW TO ADAPT TO
THE SOCIAL MOBILE CLOUD   117

Chapter 13   **Understanding Change**   119
Punctuated Equilibrium   120
Reinvention   121

Chapter 14   **Undoing Our Resistance to Learning**   123
HIDE   124
Trains, Phones, Record Players: The Cause of *What*?   135
The Crucial Skills for Twenty-First-Century Success   136
Continuous Learning: You're Either Growing or Shrinking   137

Chapter 15   **Systems Thinking**   141
Looking at the Whole   141
Shifts in Focus   144

	Tools to Assist with Optimizing Details	145
	Interactive Data Visualization	147
	Steps to Systems Thinking	148

Chapter 16	**Decision Making**	**149**
	SAFE	149
	Committing to Adapting	151
	The Continuously Iterative Business Plan	153

Chapter 17	**Seven Steps to Adaptability**	**155**
	Step 1: Why We Resist Change	155
	Step 2: Embrace Data and Analytics	156
	Step 3: Understand the Power of Social Collaboration	156
	Step 4: Why We Resist Learning	156
	Step 5: Use New Learning Tools	157
	Step 6: Learn to Use Systems Thinking	157
	Step 7: Decision Making	157

Afterword: Digital Transformation: What Will You and Your Business Look Like 10, 20, 50 Years from Now?   159

Appendix: PwC Thought Leadership on Social, Mobile, Analytics, Cloud (SMAC)   165

About the Author   217

Index   219

Preface

There's an App for That!

Why is it that people like apps so much? There is the surface answer, which is to say that apps each solve a specific problem that people have. But there is more to it than that and a good reason that "There's an app for that!" has become an exclamation of satisfaction for a growing number of smartphone adopters. Each app becomes a small demystifying revelation that arms people with whatever tool they need to become instant experts at the game, whatever the game is. There is nothing quite like that aha! moment. It gives people power, confidence, and a sense of being rewarded. And it is enjoyable because an app can add an element of fun to even the most mundane task.

Say the task is shopping for the new lawn mower you need. You download a shopping app to your smartphone, scan or key in the lawn mower's model number, and in seconds there is a list of every retailer in the vicinity selling that mower, and what it costs. Say the task is getting some signed documents copied and delivered before a meeting in 30 minutes, but you are in the car driving. Pull over for a moment, download one of a number of applications that can scan a document by using the smartphone's camera, and in seconds you have produced PDFs and e-mailed them. Running late for the airport and want to check-in, collect your boarding pass, and even pay to go through the premium service line at security? There's an app for that!

What have these tasks ultimately become? Games. Why is shopping a game? Why is sending a document a game? Why would making a flight you might otherwise miss be a game? What is a game after all? I am using the word *game* not in the narrow sense of an activity that we engage in for entertainment but in a broader sense—a set of rules that we follow to achieve objectives and to earn rewards. Our lives are full

of games when you think about it that way. Big games and little ones:
go to school, get a job, find a mate, get promoted. Navigate across
town on public transportation, make a soufflé that doesn't fall, or buy
a present for a friend that really makes him smile.

Game is just a word for a system that motivates. In thinking of our
tasks as games, we may strive to achieve them in less time or to achieve
better results. And thinking of tasks as games can make them into
ongoing cycles of improvement. You grasp one idea, particularly one
that has long been elusive to you, and pretty soon, you have another
idea. Ideas build on one another; they encourage cooperation,
collaboration, a desire to learn new things, and even the desire to
engage with one another. Making shopping into a game has been a
core tool of marketing and advertising for a century: search for the
special offer, time limited discounts, or offers only available to the first
X number of people—these are all ways of creating a system that
motivates you to purchase, in other words, a game. Companies
increasingly see that work can also be given game qualities, with
many side benefits—increased employee morale, improved productivity, and increasing quality.

And it is not just marketers and employers trying to manipulate us,
we even do this to ourselves, making our tasks and activities into
games, now with the help of apps and our ubiquitous smartphones.
We have become a nation, a globe, enamored with apps. Tens of
billions of applications have been installed by smartphone users over
the past few years. Apps have everything: easy-to-understand rules,
incredibly important functionality, flexible interaction, and instant
reward. Who wouldn't want to play this game?

I keep using the word *game*, and will continue to do so, because as
we rethink our lives, our society, and our business—specifically our
shifting mobile workforce and workplace—we must keep in mind how
technology amplifies our understanding and ability to affect human
motivations. Gamification is a process in which the implicit game that
exists in our social or business circumstance has been made explicit—
something we are rapidly doing with all of our apps. We are using
technology to make the world into a series of games, and the apps let
us track progress and compare our achievements. The apps help
make it easier to change, easier to adapt to new things, easier to win
because we are rewarded for doing these things. We are reminded
that change is constant and playful people always adapt best. And
those who adapt survive.

Let me go one step beyond survival to say adaptation to an app nation means more than surviving. It means thriving. In business, which is the lens through which this book looks at our twenty-first-century lives, we are coming into a world where any business leader armed with a smartphone can change the way business is done, the way employees and business partners interact, and the way value is created. A key to success in this new environment is in designing our businesses to use social, mobile, cloud, and the data these generate to motivate and reward employees and delight customers: to leverage the world as a game to reach our personal and business objectives.

Understanding what is happening in the new world of apps, and how gamification is changing our work and our lives, requires more than just reading about what is happening. You will need to learn through experiencing the change as well. Although the driving forces for change are technological, the change happens when behaviors shift. This is 20 percent technology and 80 percent people and process. Technologies will encourage us to change how we connect with friends or colleagues, how we shop, and how and when we work. Increasingly your success will depend on how you change your behaviors, not just whether you buy the technology.

As a business consultant, I wrote this book to serve as a prescriptive guide to help business leaders rethink their lives and build or adapt their businesses in this era of what I call the social mobile cloud. The information content in everything we do is increasing at an exponential rate and we need new tools to manage in this new world. Social technologies are expanding who we work with—beyond our immediate teams to include the whole company and beyond the company to our trading partners, customers, and even noncustomers. Mobile is the new way we get to work—or how the work gets to us, anywhere and anytime. And the cloud is where the work is done, accessible from every device and by everyone in real time.

The heart of all of this is data—generated from products and from processes—manipulated by increasingly sophisticated analytical models and provided to us in graphic visualizations to ease our comprehension and support decision making. Your business is all about the information and your job is all about what you do with that information. You may think you make a shoe, but your customers are buying an online service that allows them to track their runs and compare them with friends. You may feed people fast food, but your customers are coming into your restaurant because they can play an augmented reality game and win a mobile device from your partner. Are you selling goods or providing an experience?

Increasingly for every business it is about experience and the medium for that experience is digital. And the information about the experience is how you improve, market, and support that experience. To succeed you will have to knit together your entire ecosystem of employees, partners, and even your customers into a rich data resource and collaborative network. But don't worry. There's an app for that.

Introduction

Turning Inside Out

Each successive technology in human history has changed how we produce and consume—what today we might call the business environment—creating winners and losers. Fifteen years ago the Internet began to sweep through the marketplace, enabling a set of innovations and creating a new set of companies across many established industries. The existing businesses that owned bookstores, travel agencies, video rental businesses, and media companies were challenged by these new companies, but in many cases continued on their pre-Internet paths rather than adapting to the direction these new companies were. As a result, many companies that had been established name brands no longer exist or are shells still struggling to respond to what happened.

Today, every company I walk into as a consultant is complaining about the same challenges and asking the same set of questions about the next wave of the Internet, the next transformation, which will be driven by the social mobile cloud.

The head of customer service for a consumer software company and the chief operating officer (COO) of a large quick service restaurant chain both said a version of "I don't know who my customers are, and I don't know how to connect with them to learn what they want or how we can serve them better."

The chief executive officer (CEO) of a national recruiting and staffing organization and the chief marketing officer at a sports equipment company said, "We only engage with people in a momentary episodic way—but I know there would be so much more value created if we could connect with them [a job seeker, a purchaser of sporting goods, etc.] in an ongoing way around all of the things they do related to our service/product."

The chief information officer (CIO) of a large chemicals company and the COO of a business process outsourcing company both asked, "How can I let my employees use the mobile and social technology that they have in their personal lives for work activities without compromising security or quality?"

The senior vice president of sales at a financial services company and head of operations for a large retailer both asked, "How can I get my employees to work with one another to solve problems for our customers on the spot or collaborate to come up with better long-term solutions that we all can use?"

The general manager of a health-care products division in a large company and the head of research for an automotive manufacturer both asked, "How can I collaborate with my trading partners to extend the value of my core products and services and create more innovative and satisfying customer experiences?"

Each of these questions (and many more like them) is about how the processes of innovation, production, transaction, and consumption—processes that are all dependent on human interactions—can be improved or even radically changed through the application of a new set of digital technologies.

This book ultimately is the story of how the social mobile cloud, a combination of three new technology changes, are the core ingredients of a digital transformation in business and society, moving more quickly and cutting more deeply than any technology transformation we have ever seen. The combined impact of social technologies, the mobile Internet, and cloud computing will create incredible new business opportunities. They will also destroy unprepared companies, transform industries, and leave behind workers who are unwilling or unable to adapt. These three technologies will turn you and your company inside out.

Back in the 1990s, industry pioneers were imagining a world in which the Internet would be an everyday part of people's lives. Today, that vision has become a reality. The adoption of the Internet and the transformation of every industry and sector of our society is moving at an unprecedented speed. Now that the Internet has become a place for people, not just information, it travels with us everywhere through our mobile devices, and it is evolving into a utility as ubiquitous, reliable, and easy to use as electricity or water. Today, we experience a new consumer reality—*persistent digital engagement*—we are connected digitally to one another and to a world of information from the moment we wake up to the moment we go to sleep. Even while we sleep, a new class of products can monitor what we are doing—how well we are sleeping—transmitting data about our sleep cycles to the cloud, awaiting our analysis.

This new ubiquitous connectivity is changing our expectations as members of our communities, as citizens, and as consumers—we expect greater transparency, greater access to information, more (and faster) response and engagement, more control or at least input into decisions that affect us. In short, we expect to play a role and be an integral part in our communities, our governments, and in the companies with which we do business.

As employees, we are carrying our consumer expectations into the workplace, expecting that businesses will let us use our mobile devices, our laptops, and our social networks and will be increasingly transparent, engaging, and collaborative. The pace of change in the first wave of the Internet will be dwarfed by the changes coming in this second wave of the social mobile cloud.

There is a core factor at work in the transformation of business (and of our broader society), one that we will return to in the chapters ahead. This factor, an input into how everything in the industrial world has by necessity been organized, is the cost of communication and by extension the cost of coordination. Very simply put: As the number of people in an interaction increases, the complexity (and thus cost) of their communication increases. And the cost of communication is the largest input into the cost of coordination. When one person talks to one other person, there is a single relationship, call it A <-> B. But add just one more person and you go from one relationship to four relationships. A <-> B; B <-> C; A <-> C; and A <-> B <-> C (the dynamic when three people are together). Add a fourth person and you expand from 4 to 10 relationships—6 relationships between 2 distinct people, 3 relationships between 3 distinct people, and 1 relationship between all 4. Each collection of personalities creates a different dynamic and increases the complexity of meetings, information sharing, and decision making.

In order to scale organizations in the Industrial Age, we have had to organize innovation, production, and transactions into structured hierarchical processes—managing the interactions of each person in each process carefully so that the cost of communication and coordination did not overwhelm the system. As a result, the relationships of people inside the company to one another, and to people outside the company (trading partners, customers, regulators, and so on) have been carefully managed with walls like *customer service* and *procurement* erected to control the flow of information from the outside to the inside.

But in parallel, for hundreds of years, we have been evolving the social environment in which we interact—reducing the cost of communication and coordination through proximity and technology. Cities bring people closer together, reducing the cost of communication. The telephone reduced the impact of distance on the cost of communication. And for the past 60 years, the evolution of computing and networks has been steadily changing the cost equation.

We are now at a tipping point. For the past 100 years, hierarchical structure and prescribed process were dominant in supporting the growing scale of activity in our businesses and societies, with innovations in communication and coordination playing a lesser role. But we are now at a point where the social mobile cloud has become a more powerful force—turning our businesses inside out and exposing all of the people and processes to each other and to the outside world instead of hiding them behind walls.

What will it mean to master this new world? How will you be a leader (or at least a fast follower) in your industry? To succeed, you must understand how the coming technology changes are going to affect your company and your industry and stay ahead of your competitors in adapting to the new conditions and opportunities created by them. This book will start you on a path to making wise decisions, efficiently discriminate among possible investments, and position your business to reinvent itself and your industry. It may even help you evolve your existing business models into new ones more appropriate for this digital age.

In Chapter 5, I describe a process that I see people and organizations going through as they cope with change. I call this process ADAPT after its five steps: awareness, denial, acceptance, progress, and transformation. I hope that in reading this book, you will develop your own ability to ADAPT and also learn something about the next set of changes that will be impacting the way we live in the twenty-first century.

PART

I

The Technology of the
Social Mobile Cloud

1

A Remote Control for the World

Everything around us is about to be reinvented and reading this book is going to help you play an active role in that reinvention. The first step to becoming a reinventor is acquiring an educated, discriminating eye about technology and how it has impacted society and changed our lives over time. Knowing the players and what has happened historically is key to understanding what to look for now and to gaining access and advantage in the *social mobile cloud.*

The Three Technologies

Digital transformation—the merging of physical and digital into a new reality—is happening now, and changing how we work, play, and even how we think. Your first task is to understand the three technologies responsible for this transformation, the social mobile cloud.

Social is the people we work with, sell to, buy from, and live with— all gathered in various cooperative and collaborative groups. Social is not just online parties for teenagers. Social is also the business communities in every industry and the mechanisms that we use to work with one another. Social impacts your supply chain, your employees, your customers, and your competitors. It is also impacting your neighborhoods, your government, and the society at large. Social is also the word we use to describe a fundamental shift from hierarchical organizations and command and control business processes to peer networks and collaborative business processes.

The technology that we call social networking is simply a set of tools that make it easier to communicate and coordinate with these groups of people. Ease of communication and coordination is one of the most powerful capabilities of information technology. I am often asked by companies, "Should we block social networking sites?" But taking social networks away from your employees is a bit like taking the telephone away from them. Will people make personal calls? Yes. But using communication and coordination more effectively in everything we do is key to working more efficiently and more intelligently. And as we see in the next two technologies, making cheap communication and coordination available everywhere and all of the time has huge implications for business.

Mobile is how we get to work (or how the work gets to us), which is to say everywhere and on the move—at home, in the car, walking down the street, riding the lawn mower, at a kid's soccer game, on an airplane, and yes, occasionally in an office. Mobile means connected access to everyone and all of our businesses via key tools such as the smartphone. No business leader today can function properly without a smartphone. Increasingly, governments around the world are creating a compelling reason for us to have smartphones as citizens as well. Smartphones will move beyond communication and will even replace the other two things we have long carried in our pockets: our keys and our wallets. This smart digital device will soon unlock doors and pay the bill at a store or a restaurant. They will also become ubiquitous scanners, sensing every aspect of the physical and digital environments around us—informing our purchase decisions, helping us to make friends, and warning us of danger.

The *cloud* is where the office is, the new place we work. It is computing as a utility—infrastructure "somewhere" that enables us to do everything. It is the connective tissue that makes communication and coordination possible. We don't have to carry all knowledge around with us or even know where it is stored—we just need to have access to a search engine. We don't need cash in our pockets, we just need a connection to our bank accounts. And the cloud makes it ridiculously easy for any business or individual to create new digital extensions to existing products and services, or to create new ways for customers or vendors to interact. From the perspective of the individual, the cloud is unlimited computing power that is on tap anytime, from anywhere, ready to answer our questions, to store information, to connect us to colleagues or friends, or to help us through any process. However, companies need to understand the subtleties among the private, public, and hybrid clouds about which we will talk later. Specific business reasons may compel your business to operate a private cloud—but the greatest advantages come when you are able to embrace computing as a utility.

Digital transformation occurs when the physical and the digital worlds join forces, when the *social mobile cloud*—our contemporary state of being—allows us to rethink how we do everything. We walk through life with our smartphones as a kind of remote control. With a smartphone in your hand, you are carrying a device that works on everything. Everything. Knowledge, communication, access, payment, and increasingly the control of mechanical and electronic devices around us are all being aggregated into your smartphone. Everything you do, or want to do, you do by clicking on an app on this remote control. That is the social mobile cloud. That is already business today, and it will impact our whole society tomorrow. And that remote control is also your game controller, adding a sense of fun, a way to measure accomplishment, and a means to compare, compete, and cooperate with friends or colleagues.

As successful as some new Internet generation companies have been, traditional companies are often still in denial that the social mobile cloud has transformed their industries. While some have accepted the new reality (and have task forces studying how their businesses must change), few companies have gone on to radically reimagine their businesses. The biggest changes challenging existing companies and their old ways are still to come as we learn to develop and transform and as we understand the full implications of the social mobile cloud.

Lessons from the History of the Internet

The most important thing to remember as you read this brief history and current marketplace assessment is that the strategies of the successful technology companies are cumulative. In Chapter 5, I will explain the process called ADAPT that can help you navigate the changes ahead. Grounding your own ADAPT strategy in an understanding of the past will help you benefit from the cumulative, experimental approach that companies have gone through over the last few decades. It is a process that depends on a certain degree of scientific method—hypothesize, experiment, learn, and improve. But in order to experiment in the most efficient, cost effective, and productive manner, it is imperative to know which technologies to embrace.

The timing for understanding the marketplace couldn't be more urgent. The last cycle was all about what was going to happen, a collective scramble to envision what the world might look like once there were hundreds of millions of people online. This time around there is no need to predict. There are not only hundreds of millions of people online but they also have mobile access to the Internet. Now it is about what has already happened and understanding the implications. Embracing these technologies to reinvent your business is not about taking avant-garde risk, it is about surviving as a business. Governments are being transformed; new ways to run our society are being developed. Competitiveness as individuals and organizations depends on not just the ability to grasp these changes but also the speed with which you do so.

One example that crystallizes the business environment today and serves as a wake-up call for all businesses in all industries is what has happened to newspapers. A critical part of the business of newspapers depended on classified advertising. The very name of these sections calls to mind the difference between predigital and digital marketplaces. Classification systems are necessary when information is presented in a linear format, such as print. Classified advertising provided newspapers with an enormously important part of their revenue models—anyone in a community who wanted to sell something, buy something, hire someone, rent an apartment, and so on, could list the item (for a fee) in the correct section of a printed publication, reaching interested members of a community.

But the Internet challenged this model by allowing people to find and connect with one another around these transactions more efficiently. When a variety of companies emerged in the marketplace to offer job listings, apartment listings, and everything else that had been in the classifieds section, every major newspaper should have seen the writing on the wall for this core source of revenue.

Every major newspaper saw it happening, every major newspaper had deeper pockets than the set of upstart companies entering their markets, yet the incumbents failed to create a competitor. Instead, most publishers sat back and watched a small group of start-up Internet companies destroy the core section of their product that had traditionally paid the overhead for the entire newspaper.

Ask yourself why they allowed that to happen. Ask yourself how important it is for you to be able to spot the next threat to your industry. Ask yourself how important it is now to have a team in place, at any company, in any industry, whose stated goal is to find a way to destroy their own company (or at least the existing way of doing business). Ask yourself if that team, with that mission, isn't the key to reinvention versus obsolescence.

While you are answering this question, be aware that most organizations are bad at innovation. That team whose mission is to destroy your company will likely need some external assistance. Consider how innovation is occurring now in the smartphone industry. The makers of smartphone operating systems have enabled others to invent the apps, to create the path of innovation. A lot of money is wasted experimenting on new ideas for apps, but not the money of the companies who make the phones or the operating systems. These companies have developed *co-creation ecosystems* and they are marshaling external innovation to reinvent their products and company. As part of the design of these ecosystems, the smartphone manufacturers benefit from successful innovation while being sheltered from the risk of failed experiments. Billions of dollars of other people's money is now rapidly improving the smartphone customer experience and increasing the desirability of these products.

You might be saying that the concept of creating an ecosystem lends itself to technology companies more readily than to other organizations. How do you design for external innovation if you are selling clothing? Can external innovation help a police department? However, if you focus too hard on the specific goods being manufactured, the means of production, or the services being provided, you are missing a key point about how markets are evolving and what you will have to do to remain competitive.

Every organization in our society is being transformed by technology in the sense that technology is changing the way we connect to markets; the way products are developed, marketed, purchased, and supported; and the way that we work and live together. Every connection point between you and the people and systems that you use is being transformed by technology.

For example, consider how your customers interact with your brand, and the say you allow them to have in design. Are you closed to customer input about the next version of your product? Or do you survey your customers or run focus groups? How connected to customers can your product development process become? Openness is the main operating system for the social mobile cloud. External innovation in this case might mean using social networking specialists to invite your customers to contribute their ideas directly into your product development process, inviting them all the way into a core part of your business.

Or imagine that police department I just mentioned. What could we achieve by encouraging citizens to record and report on police conduct rather than prosecuting them for doing so (as many states now do)? Can we make our cities safer by improving the accountability of our public servants? Can we restore trust in public institutions and reward the best police by calling out those few individuals that give the service a bad name through graft, abusive behavior, or negligence?

The History Lesson: Big Picture Thinkers Survive the Game

From 1994 to 2000, the early pioneers of the World Wide Web were like contestants on a reality TV show in which individuals are eliminated as the show progresses. The people who survived, successfully cooperated and collaborated, and created harmony with the elements were people who could take on any game challenge with confidence, but at the same time be discriminating about what was important for survival and what was not. Greed on the Web didn't help, just like power mongering and cockiness when marooned on an island doesn't help.

During the early to mid-1990s, pundits declared that the Internet would be an enormously disruptive force in the broader economy. Companies and entire industries would be transformed, consumer behavior would shift, and entirely new business opportunities would emerge.

Then something went horribly wrong. A long period of tech industry expansion (1980–2000), quickly became the dot-com bubble. Overhyped companies promising to become empires just because they could manage to deliver pet food or gift baskets collapsed or radically refocused into much more modest businesses.

In the midst of frenzied investment into this future, two small facts were overlooked:

First, it takes time for technologies to be broadly adopted and for consumers to shift their basic patterns of consumption. The expectations of financial markets that these businesses would create avatar-dependent consumers (or any number of radical ideas) in a matter of fiscal quarters were simply unrealistic. Just building the fiber optic infrastructure required for high-speed Internet access to become ubiquitous took longer than that, even though jackhammers were digging up sidewalks and city streets all over the country as fast as possible.

Second, the mechanisms needed to operate these new markets with all of their new interrelationships were still being invented and would take time to mature.

These two factors were juxtaposed against the short attention span of the financial markets. The result: Excitement over the potential long-term impact of these technologies encouraged an investment cycle that had nowhere to go but crash. The immediate gratification expectation simply far exceeded the tangible impact of the technologies. Capital was also inefficiently allocated into too many firms. Because capital was too readily available, firms were merely mimicking one another, creating far too much supply for slower growing demand.

Early on in the development of a new technology, there is always excitement about its potential. Companies engaged in this new business area are able to attract press coverage beyond their relative merit because innovation is perceived to be more newsworthy than established technologies and businesses. Unfortunately, publicity can sometimes outpace the development of markets for the new technology. The resulting crash sends the media and weaker business off to look for new opportunities.

But for technologies that are destined to prove themselves and eventually have a real impact, there is a steady rise into a mature and sustainable marketplace. These companies are likely to become successful and highly valued corporations.

Applying this to the Internet sector as a whole, we see the cycle from 1994 to 2000 as a period of steep, hyped-up rise, collapsing with the dot-com bubble into a deep trough of disillusionment. Now that we are collectively disillusioned about retail investing in the tech sector, it may be hard to imagine that not so long ago we overlooked a hype cycle, a term many today consider obvious.

But remember that technological innovation and adoption are a steady, cumulative phenomenon. So the important message to take away from the hype cycle of the 1990s is to focus on what happened to the best companies, the ones that survived the plateau of productivity: Many of them have gone on to become world-leading businesses. Knowing which companies survived the financial market storms in the

1990s is your first step to having a trained eye for worthy technology players. Several companies were created in the Internet boom cycle starting in 1994 that are today highly valued and productive companies, despite the overvaluation and subsequent crash of the dot-com era.

Just as the market had overvalued and overinvested in the Internet sector in the 1990s, a period of undervaluation and underinvestment followed, even though the underlying fundamentals driving the value of many of these companies continued to develop at a steady pace. This is also typical of the financial markets, which tend to follow a collapsed greed cycle with a fear cycle.

Many of these new companies succeeded because they recognized the critical factor that technology had come to play in their industries where traditional companies denied or ignored the new role that technology was playing in redefining how markets functioned, product and service definition, customer expectations, and even how the companies were organized internally or operated in conjunction with partners.

It is especially hard for companies in nontechnology industries to grasp the importance of embracing technology in transforming businesses. Many companies have entirely outsourced technical expertise, thinking that it is unimportant since they are a manufacturer or a retailer or shipping company and not a software company. But it would be a mistake to underestimate the strategic importance of the social mobile cloud. These technologies have a tendency to change everything about how a market and an industry function.

The other characteristic to look out for is in your own behavior and that of your colleagues. I mentioned earlier that this is 80 percent about people, not technology. One of the most detrimental side effects for thought leaders in business is to throw out the whole concept of a technological evolution, or even revolution, during that stock market fear cycle I mentioned, the one that follows the greedy hype cycle. But it is about how you shift behaviors, develop skills, and put new processes in place that will determine whether you and your colleagues will successfully navigate your business to adapt to the social mobile cloud.

Don't fall into naysaying (which later I'll call the Denial stage of the ADAPT process) and believe you can return to pre-Internet business models. It will be the attitude that renders your business obsolete. When you evaluate companies that have been successful and all the indicators of a true industry re-inventor are there, recognize that people and their behaviors and adaptability have made the difference. As a businessperson you already know this in the following corollary: If you want to be somewhere solid in five years, you better start now.

If you need reminding that the Internet business model is here to stay, consider just how many examples there are. It's no longer the exception, but rather the rule: Think about how the encyclopedia industry has been reinvented. What else is silently becoming less important or disappearing? How often do you still use those yellow-paged books the phone companies drop by our doors? How frequently do you walk into a bank versus even five years ago? How many of your bills does the mail carrier still deliver? When was the last time you spoke to a travel agent? Have you bought any record albums or watched any videotapes recently? Have you mailed any letters? Which brand of film is best is another question we hardly ask now—because many of us don't use film anymore. Digital transformation has forever changed all of these things.

And this is just the beginning, because now it is not just digital formats replacing analog and the Internet connecting us to one another. Now it is about using an expanding array of portable digital devices to access the Internet from anywhere, anytime, for both personal and business use and an integration of digital into everything else. The social mobile cloud is the way we are all starting to live and play, and it is the way we will all do business.

Build for the Social Mobile Cloud

Think about how to build your business for the social mobile cloud. You don't want to add social mobile cloud functionality later. If you do, you'll be significantly behind competitors, and catching up might be impossible. Your digital engagement capabilities—whether with employees, trading partners, or customers—will always be piecemeal, you will be in constant need of upgrading, which translates to far greater expense than it would cost to do the whole job at the outset. Wait and you will spend more and still come away with a less functional result. For your industry, ask yourself if there is a way your competitors could create a barrier to entry by leveraging the social mobile cloud. Can you get there first?

Our remote control smartphone will have an app for absolutely every function in our personal and professional lives. The word *phone* itself is quickly becoming some linguistic evolution curiosity—like "dial a number" or "tape record." We'll continue to use the word *phone* despite the declining use of such devices to make calls although you can expect our children and grandchildren to have no idea why we call it a phone. Most of the time we won't use these pocket computers to make calls, we'll be using them to interact with information systems.

We are in the midst of an enormous transformation in the human-machine interface, precipitated by these new remote control smartphones. The revolution of windows, menus, and mice that defined the second generation of computing (graphical user interfaces instead of command line instructions) and made it broadly accessible is rapidly being replaced by a third generation. Touch interfaces, virtual "physics" on the screens, and immersive computing environments where computation, sensors, and voice communications are embedded in everything around us will make the computer disappear, blending with everything with which we interact. In 10 years, the computer mouse will seem just as quaint as the punch card that was once used to program computers. We'll simply talk to the computers all around us, and they will organize themselves to best meet our requests.

The Time Is *Now*

The process of setting up a business to be functional for a social mobile cloud workforce, with mobile business partners and mobile customers—which is an imperative, not an option—requires starting now. Remember, all technology deployment, companywide policy setting, and learning curves take time. In fact, *every* part of your business will have to change to make your company ready for the social mobile cloud way of doing business in your industry. If you wait, someone other than you will invent the app that will destroy your business.

In part, the social mobile cloud revolution snuck up on us because we were distracted by the housing bubble, sovereign debt crises, and other political and economic problems. But much more pertinent is that our new way of functioning is coming on fast and furiously because the underlying technology is moving so much faster than we have experienced in past booms. And the key is that because it involved so many more people, the phenomenon of hitting critical mass naturally occurred quickly.

To fully understand the implications of the social mobile cloud for all businesses, you need to understand how that critical mass point occurred and how the social mobile cloud boom came to involve so many more people. And to understand that, I will need to go a bit deeper into the technological trends of social networks and cloud computing.

Social Networking Is the Fastest Growing Technology Ever

Mobile may be growing like wildfire, but social networks are growing even faster, and in fact are the catalysts for mobile (hence, my insistence on using social mobile cloud instead of mobile Internet). Social networks are the watercoolers of the virtual mobile workforce. Peers in a workplace do not collaborate well, or form successful teams, until they can know one another in a somewhat personal way. Social networks humanize the mobile workforce.

And the virtual watercooler point is merely stressing the importance of social networks for internal corporate functionality. The social network technology, these communities, also supply all businesses with a mechanism for marketing, advertising, public relations, purchasing, sales, potential partnering, and even funding!

In short, because of social networking, we are all developing online social peripheral vision, which is the impressionistic understanding of what is going on in the social networks—what is going on with the people in every aspect of our lives—even at times when we are not directly engaged. That awareness, which ultimately means the intent to engage with people at some point, is now an integral part of the lives of your employees, your business partners, and your customers. It means that you are more connected to people than you have ever been. That connectedness leads to openness—sharing ideas instead of hoarding, responding to a group's articulated needs and desires. *Share everything* is the hallmark quality of the social mobile cloud, a quality you absolutely need to embrace in your business culture to survive.

In the book publishing business, social networking can prove viability for a book deal through an author building a following. If the number of connections surpasses the average number of books traditionally sold, that author may have leverage in negotiations. In the same breath, the e-book is becoming front and center in terms of how people will read and share books. The trend of e-books, the tablets for which are now sold by many book retailers, proves the relationship between the social, transferrable quality of commodities today and our ingrained mobility. Who will travel on subways or airplanes carrying heavy books when they can pack 10 novels on an e-book reader?

A related trend is happening in the television industry. Television networks now gauge a show's success using social media. The number of social network followers for any given show vies with the traditional rating system in terms of providing a tangible indicator of a show's viability and success. In every business we can evaluate the social engagement with our product and brand and learn how things are going. Was the new product release received well by the market? Why wait until the quarterly financial results come out when your customers are talking about it now?

The Cloud: The Connective Tissue

All technologies in the social mobile cloud work together, so the infrastructure and applications must be built together. You must fund your ADAPT process for social and mobile and cloud technologies together.

Think of the cloud as infrastructural, like the electricity grid. When you turn on a light, you don't need to know how it works, where the power is coming from, or need special lightbulbs, switches, or knowledge of operations. You don't have the grid in your office building, you don't pay for the infrastructure except indirectly through your usage. If this were an economy and power structure of 100 years ago, the government might have even appropriated cloud technology, and it wouldn't be private technology companies owning that infrastructure but public utility companies.

There are four technologies that are rapidly standardizing which create the new reality of cloud computing. Servers, networks, storage, and software are converging on a set of industry accepted practices such that companies are all building data centers that pretty much look like one another. And the best part is that as a business user you don't need to understand any of this—it is all just out there somewhere and you can connect.

The cloud allows us to shift how we think about the IT department and the role of the CIO. IT operations are declining in importance in what you need to worry about in your business—but don't confuse this with needing to understand IT. There is still an enormous role for technology understanding in your business—but the need is for a different skill set. Instead of managing the systems of IT—data centers, networks, and equipment—the CIO's job is increasingly that of a business solutions broker. How can the goals of business continuity, data security, and increased business functionality be best served through orchestrating solutions in the social mobile cloud? How can IT be the enabler for business transformation? Can IT change the way every functional department works across the enterprise making us more efficient, more capable, and even happier?

Using the cloud to run any size business is an easy habit to form because it cuts technology costs as you adopt, innovate, and transform your business. (Perhaps I should have started this entire book with that sentence!)

In simplest terms, cloud computing means you no longer have to own expensive technology that serves, archives, and communicates. You pay a metered rental fee, and are hosted, precisely like utilities. You use mobile devices (sometimes called "edge" devices) to access this data, with very little persistence in the computer we hold in our hands, and everything remaining in the cloud. In Chapter 4, I'll go into detail about the technological benefits of the cloud, such as instant access to cross referenced databases on the Internet, analytics-driven data mining, synchronizing data across any device regardless of retrieval location, and literally having your entire marketplace and supply chain just a few taps away on your smartphone.

Digital transformation is the end of the tyranny of brick and mortar and the rise of the social mobile cloud. People have talked and talked about how brick-and-mortar retail will fall to the Internet, but people have also been talking about the death of radio for 20 years now. Now that the Internet is in everyone's hands what is actually happening is that mobile devices are transforming the experience of brick-and-mortar businesses through information on demand and social engagement. There is a fallacy in thinking that it is possible to live all of life on the Internet, that we are capable of being online beings that use the globe as a village. This is an extremist point of view held by some technologists. You need to remember that people live locally, not globally, and the businesses that do best are ones that find a way to engage people in both the physical and online worlds, and have both of those worlds tailored to local underpinnings. It is much like the old saying "think globally, act locally."

In the same breath, the challenge is to understand that every business can span the globe instantly but must be expressed in locally relevant ways. When we get to the cloud technology chapter, you'll understand why the Internet search has become so pervasive. When you think cloud, think search. Key in what you want and you access it, whether it is the nearest cafe, the lyrics to an old song, a map of a remote African village, or the ability to share an editable PDF document with a simple link on a social network. Now take it one step further in your thinking: Yes, you can have customers across the globe, but tailoring your offering to their local existence will be key. Naturally, there will be certain needs, like searching for the nearest cafe, which lend themselves to being local, while other needs, such as lyrics to an old song, are global, without the need for a location. Understanding how both needs go together will enable you to fully engage in the social mobile cloud.

By "fall to the Internet," it's important to note, again, that I mean to emphasize wholesale reinvention, not just retail: everything we do in a physical world—school, work, and play. Front end and back end. There is no longer so much of a separation. The expression *plork*, which is play + work = plork, was coined to describe a very real feeling that people are having about their lives. As we move from sustaining ourselves to thriving the next step is self-actualization and a natural state is to actually enjoy the work we are doing.

In part, the social mobile cloud will have a more profound effect on society than the rise of the Internet because it brings the Internet into more people's hands, in more places, and for more time (try all the time). There are all sorts of implications of what a place is, which I'll get to in the individual discussions of social networks and the cloud. These are all multipliers on impact.

Buy a Smartphone Now

Ultimately, the most important concept of social networks and cloud computing technology to integrate into your thinking, as a consumer as well as a businessperson, is that the smartphone is the remote control for your personal life, as well as for every interaction with human and machine in the workplace.

In Chapter 5, I will detail the ADAPT process, but here I'll provide a little bit of foreshadowing—acceptance is the first step if you don't want to fall behind in the game. Accepting the reality of being mobile and therefore constantly accessible and accountable, engaged in social networking, and operating via an offsite cloud infrastructure, isn't something that will happen without some work. In order to fully grasp the implications and how to properly ADAPT the social mobile cloud into your business and industry, start from the consumer point of view.

If you don't have one already, purchase a smartphone and start using it. In the future no one is going to leave home without this remote control for their life. Especially because the smartphone will become our wallets and our keys in addition to being a ubiquitous lifeline to information and people.

In terms of other immediate technological acquisitions, also purchase a tablet if you can. You need to see how the cloud, and lightweight mobile tools, with enticing tactile and visual elements, and of course connected to the Internet, are changing the way we function. And when you use the cloud to access the same data across your computer, smartphone, and tablet, the endless possibilities of the social mobile cloud become instantly clear. People say they're addicted to their smartphones for good reason. People are addicted to their traditional television remote controls, after all, which have a fraction of the functionality of a smartphone, in a universe infinitesimally smaller than the global Internet.

There is no turning back. These trends are here to stay, and are the foundation of your thinking as I move on to the discussion of individual technologies in social, mobile, and cloud, both in terms of existing and future applications. By the time you get to the second section of this book, the implications for businesses and society, you will be able to start creating a special team, one inside your company whose stated goal is to figure out how to destroy (reinvent!) your company and industry.

CHAPTER 2

Social Means Connected

Compete with Yourself, Collaborate with Others

In Chapter 3, I will talk about how to use mobile devices to stay connected and how the cloud provides the infrastructure to be connected. But what does it mean to be connected? Social technologies take the most basic building blocks of human society and exponentially accelerate them. By eliminating the limitations of time and space that have previously governed how we organize our interactions, new software systems radically transform what people can achieve together. Embedding these new capabilities into your organizations, your products, and how you engage with your markets will be essential to your success.

Cheap computer systems and networks have reduced the cost of communication to practically zero. It is no longer necessary to own a printing press or a broadcasting tower to deliver your ideas to a marketplace. Social media takes advantage of this change and gives everyone the ability to publish ideas—blogs and specialized content sharing sites all create the opportunity to deliver your idea to the vast audience using the Internet.

But social media is only a beginning point, not an end point. And if you are only talking about social media in your business, you are missing the forest for the trees. Having every person in the world as simply a broadcasting tower would result in cacophony if there were no way to organize people and ideas, and this is where the power of social technologies really becomes interesting.

The Social Network

The step beyond social media is the social network—adding to the ability to communicate is the ability to organize that communication around people. Everyone you know, and everyone you want to know, categorized into groups and organized by how you want to interact with the people in the group. Social networks are a first step in going beyond communication to coordination. Later in this chapter we'll discuss specialized tools for specific kinds of coordination. At a basic level, however, social networking offers a medium to more readily connect social media to the specific segment of the global audience who cares about a specific message. It could be 10 people, just your close friends, or 10 million who share a passion to change a policy or overthrow a dictator. In each case, the tool simply creates the possibility of coordination and it is the use of the tool, the actions of its users, which determine its purpose.

Remember the remote control from Chapter 1—when you push a button on a remote control, you do so with the expectation of getting a specific reaction, direct feedback of a particular nature. When you are using a social network, you are developing the behaviors behind the buttons of your remote. If you collect your family and friends, your social network might be about the events and ideas that are important to you for personal reasons. If your network is full of business connections, the content will be about your company or your industry. Who you connect with should align with what you connect about. There will be more discussion on what happens when these elements are not aligned later in the chapter.

Now, the beauty of social networks is that they can fit a lot more people than you could ever imagine into a single room, thereby giving you access to more people than you ever imagined. And the tools are becoming more and more sophisticated to allow you to connect with lots of different people with whom you'll share lots of different things. And social networks really shine because your interaction is highly productive and efficient and personally rewarding.

Imagine being at a business cocktail party and working the room. You've done this 100 times. You need to get to know people and have them know you. You give your spiel over and over as you meet people. It takes hours. But now consider the same scenario in a social network: You give your spiel once and put it online. It takes moments. Better yet, you ask a compelling question because the key to getting people to engage in a social network is to ask people things, not tell them things. When you make declarations, there is no opening for people to talk to you. You ask questions, you get answers, conversations start, relationships form. Once you ask the question, you wait for responses while you do other things. The responses you get are the equivalent of a salesperson finding qualified prospects. Even if you're not selling something in the moment, the people who engage with you are proactively interested in you, as opposed to being polite merely because you approached them at a cocktail party.

So now imagine the nature of this level of interaction, including weeding out disinterested parties, as it would apply to different business functions. It is limitless, efficient, enjoyable, productive, open, and friendly.

The personal social club aspect of social networking that you've heard the most about really is just the beginning. All communication and selling will happen via social networks, as well as all interaction with employees, business partners, supply chains, and customers. If you are not operating your business including social networks right now, you are seriously behind. And you are missing out on joyful interaction. Really. Social networks add to your quality of business life. Think about how much time you spend alone in your work, needing or wanting some kind of feedback but not having access to it; or can only access by scheduling and attending meetings, which take a lot of time, even if they're valuable. When we think, our brains look for external stimuli all the time, to help us process. Now that ability to process is a click away, whether it is to bat around an idea with a supplier, or to wonder out loud if customers would appreciate your bundling together two products that you sell.

So what happens when your personal world and your work world collide online? The permeability of our social networks will be an increasingly challenging problem and not only because of what we do but also because of what the people around us do with these tools. No matter how diligent you are in keeping your personal interests confined online to appropriate friends and family, anything about you can be published online at any time using any of these tools and is then a quick search away from a professional colleague trying to find out more about you.

Have you attended a political rally recently? Did someone take your picture? Did someone else recognize you and add your name to the image when it was uploaded to an advocacy website? Now imagine a search for your name broadcasts to the world your political opinions, and it doesn't distinguish among searchers. Friends, family, business colleagues, and customers alike can discover your allegiances with whatever consequences may come from that disclosure. Does your employer have a policy prohibiting employees from taking a public advocacy role on political issues? With social networks, every moment is potentially a public moment.

A few practical realities emerge. In the near term, depending on your line of work, you may need to be more discrete about where you go, who you are with, and what you do if the disclosure of those facts will negatively impact your personal reputation or your business. But in the long run our society, and our business community, is becoming more tolerant of our individual differences and preferences. Diversity in religious beliefs, ethnicity, sexual preference, political party membership, and many other differences between us are increasingly accepted, and in the best of circumstances, embraced as bringing greater opportunity to collaborate, learn, and solve problems together.

Our new capacity to connect to one another and to communicate more deeply about ourselves will necessarily lead to greater authenticity—a greater degree of honesty with everyone in our lives about who we truly are. What we do with that new reality—whether we use it to persecute people who are different from ourselves or instead use it to celebrate the differences that make us stronger together—will ultimately say more about us than what has been published about us. But the transition will be bumpy. Expect moments of embarrassment or worse.

Despite these challenges, you need to build your business around social tools. Not allowing your employees to use social networks is the equivalent of not allowing them to have telephones. Business is all about communication—why wouldn't you want to equip your workforce with the most powerful communication tools available? Yes, there are risks and they must be managed. *Start with a thorough business communications policy* (not a social media policy) and education. Let everyone know what they could do that would get them into trouble. And what they can do to get themselves out of trouble. Every e-mail, every phone call, every discussion in a public (or even in a private) forum could become a part of someone's social broadcast. Think about all the ways your business communicates internally with partners and with customers, and consider what happens when those communications become a part of an online social network—whether you intend them to or not.

Chapter 3 discusses the mobile phone and its role in digital transformation, but it is worthwhile to mention here the tight connection between social and mobile. Even if you are sitting chained to a desk, every time you go to a social network, the people you connect with can be anywhere and at anytime in their day (or night). Social and mobile are about engaging with a dispersed population. You may be sitting at a desk, but the supplier who answers your social networking question may be between flights, sitting at an airline gate, and answering from his smartphone.

The mobile device is also a sensor—capturing sounds and images from the hundreds of millions of locations where people are working and playing, and then broadcasting those recordings to the social mobile cloud. Social networks are growing faster than mobile tools, but have become a catalyst for mobile technology growth. Social networks are the reason that there are hundreds of millions of people that want to be online all the time—sharing their experiences.

When you start using a smartphone, the first phenomenon you will notice is that there is no such thing as idle time anymore if you don't want idle time. Order a sandwich at a deli, and while you're waiting in line for it you can answer a few work e-mails or texts, or read stock news, or check your calendar, weather, flight delays, or employee interaction on a social network. The list goes on and on and is only limited by the number of apps on your phone. This can be a negative thing as well—don't forget to make time for daydreaming—one of the most important ways we reflect and innovate. But the mobile device provides the choice.

You may have already decided that your business needs an overhaul. The good news is that social networks deliver potential customers for a fraction of the cost of traditional marketing methods. Your employees are capable of using social networks to solve problems faster, increase quality, and improve their satisfaction. Your supply chain has never had a better chance to communicate more effectively, to eliminate error and waste; arguably not even by using multimillion dollar business intelligence (BI) enterprise software, driven by analytics. What social networks give everyone is access. Social networks are accessible, disarming, and highly usable. So the result? No one obviates the system. Everyone wants in. Everyone *is* in. Remember, too, that every single one of those people is a citizen, a customer, and an employee. Really make sure that last sentence imprints; it is the key to making the most of social networks.

Discoverability is a term associated with peer communications networks. Simply put, it enables people to seek out other people who really need to know something. If you are a part of a social network you can search for other people interested in the same topics you care about. Discoverability is the capacity of a system to respond to intent—you know what you want to find, and you are using the system to make that discovery.

There is another term associated with the advantage of social networks: serendipity. Serendipity is the flip side of discoverability. It is what happens when you put like-minded people in the same room and brainstorm. Instead of intent you have interest—you don't know what you want to find but you know roughly the subject. A software system allows employees to create profiles of themselves and what they're working on and interested in, and then forms clusters of people around those interests.

Discoverability and serendipity are the twin gifts of the social network to your enterprise. They lead to collaboration, new work methods, enhanced productivity, product development, interactive marketing, and so on.

Co-Creation

If you were to simply stop at social media and social networking though, you would still be missing the essential element that the social mobile cloud has introduced into our society, radically changing how we live, work, and play. Social media and social networks are building blocks for systems that change the way we create—sometimes called social production, or more commonly co-creation. It is when you add a purpose, an objective, to social interactions that a real transformation results. These tools are not just paving the way for mild improvements in old ways of interacting; they contain the capability to fundamentally change the way we interact. Businesses must design systems that encourage collaboration, providing the right incentives inherent in the way the technology is deployed to support people in learning to collaboratively reach desired outcomes.

I've touched briefly on how social networks are the watercooler of the mobile workforce, and that bonding personally is what enables people to work together in teams. But that's just the beginning. The interaction is not just downtime driven. The nature of sharing information in our knowledge economy is what leads to collaboration. Once employees are untethered (see Chapter 3), rewarded by results, and empowered to be a spokesperson of his or her employer, collaboration becomes an imperative. The more people work in physical solitude, the more they will collaborate via social networks. And that's merely the psychological nature of gregarious beings. While the industrial economy demanded individual effort on an assembly line, the knowledge economy itself demands collaboration.

The design imperative for your business processes must be to encourage collaboration, encourage information sharing, and reward contribution. Incentive design is the process by which you examine the network of stakeholders, the types of interactions they might have, and build rewards into your processes to support the outcomes you desire. By rewards I don't mean just monetary (although that can be important). Consider the rewards of recognition, satisfaction at a job well-done, entertainment, or the feeling of having made a positive contribution to a worthy cause. All of these can have as much (or in some cases more) impact on a contributor than money.

Compete with Yourself

Let me talk about competition for one moment so you know where it fits in to this era. The credo of the social mobile cloud world is to compete with yourself and collaborate with others. There should be a team inside your company, whose mission is to destroy your company. That is you competing with yourself. That's why it's critical that such a team be built properly, with the right budget to ADAPT, with leadership, a stake for everyone on the team, and whole company support. There is no better way to gain competitive edge—never mind saving your company from obsolescence—than self-competition. We were taught to compete with ourselves and not compare ourselves to others, as kids. We know it as parents. Apply that concept to your business.

At the same time, design systems that allow your employees to reach outside the four walls of your business and collaborate with others. There are a lot of smart people outside of your organization, and a lot of them would be very happy to help you achieve your goals. Their motivations are not unlike those of your employees—they seek recognition, entertainment, that sense of satisfaction at having contributed to something wonderful, and sometimes even financial rewards. They bring new thinking, different skills, and a much broader perspective to your company's challenges.

Sign Up for a Social Network Today—on Your New Smartphone

Before you read another sentence, go sign up for a social network. Just sign up for a personal account. Leave the business implications aside for right now. You will learn about the business application by osmosis. I am shocked at the number of businesspeople who tell me that they do not use social networks. Especially the ones with children who should at least be connecting and understanding what their children are doing online. And once you are using social networks for personal matters, the business application will emerge. The nature of our consumer and business online personas today is such that everything you do with the social mobile cloud will entangle them with one another. Internet search (not to mention hundreds of social media analytics platforms) guarantees that this will happen. But when you sign up for these services and become a social network consumer, you will, in a matter of weeks, understand your own customers and employees better than you ever have.

In terms of customers and consumer behavior, while you are playing around on social networks, looking for "friends," search out subject matter you are interested in as a consumer. Really examine how the buying process is changing. There are so many new inputs to awareness, purchase decisions, and the choice of the point of sale . . . even new opportunities to engage during purchases and new levels of what happens postpurchase in terms of support and advocacy. You need to offer these opportunities to your own customers and track how consumers behave when sharing their opinions.

To that end, also familiarize yourself with sites designed to share specialized media like videos or presentations. On these sites, where people all have their own television stations and newspapers in the form of blogs, the ability to share information, reviews, and news is unlimited. Add mobile technology as the key tool to this mix and you can easily imagine an interactive avatar as an app that will be your personal shopper, assimilating information from hundreds of product reviews, distilling that data down to an intelligent choice for you as a consumer, based on articulated and even unarticulated preferences. Perhaps avatar versions of journalists will be the norm for newspaper reviewers and columnists over the next couple of years.

Pay attention to that last sentence. I'm not contemplating futuristic visions. I'm talking about now. Social networks are essentially a range of online activities that connect individuals to one another, bypassing the anointed mouthpieces of media giants. Your company's ability to offer those activities is a key barometer of your ability to survive.

To understand the state of social networks in terms of social network commerce, study the new shopping and coupon sites, in particular ones exploring the newest category of collaborative online consumer behavior, "social shopping"—the electronic version of coupon clipping. Here is an example of the new game: A merchant agrees to offer consumers a discount on products or services if a certain number of people buy in. There is a special of the day for each town. A website acts as the "stock exchange" for the service. When you, as a consumer go to the site you learn what the daily deal for your local region is, and you decide whether you want to buy in. Discounts are steep, anything from half price off a hang-gliding lesson, to discounts at your local bowling alley. If enough people buy in, the discount is on. There's a ticker that tells you how many people have bought in, whether the deal is officially on, and a countdown of how many hours, minutes, and seconds are left to buy into the deal.

A number of companies are also in the early stages of creating mobile payment systems. The idea is that you have an app on your smartphone that is your stored value, your money, and you click on it to pay for something at participating merchants. These apps connect consumers to special offers, drive them to spend more at specific merchants, and generate an enormous amount of data that companies can analyze to understand preferences, behaviors, beliefs, and habits (and ultimate influence them).

That we will eventually stop using plastic and paper money is a given. I'll go into detail about the reinvention of money, MONEY 2.0, in Chapter 11. What is important here, in terms of social network commerce, is that over the next few years, buying products and services in social networks using digital stored value, often corporate sponsored value such as reward points, will be the norm. You need to access consumers in this manner. And we will get to strategies for doing just that in the second section. Chapters 5 through 8 describe the essential issues, strategies, and business implications.

One more important lesson you'll learn by playing around on social networks is how serendipity comes into play: Being in the right place at the right time absolutely gives you business opportunity. Think of it as the old real estate credo—location, location, location— applied to business in the social mobile cloud. Why is a retailer's location in real estate important? Because if you're in the middle of a heavily trafficked area, you'll get foot traffic—a passerby deciding on the spur of the moment to check out what you have to offer. If you create a vibrant energy, then maybe a crowd will form. Once a few people crowd around, more people are drawn in.

Apply that principle to the serendipity of social networks. If you have a presence in popular social networks and a subject comes up that's pertinent to your business, you can jump in with an offer. And that serendipity isn't entirely by chance. You can find social network groups with interests and psychographic profiles that lend themselves to serendipity. Perhaps you've heard the expression "you make your own luck." Well, it applies to social networks and what you have to do to succeed in them. "Promiscuity is good, exclusivity is bad" while being a bad idea in your personal relationships is an important principle to adopt in online spaces. Share, and hope that those you share with also share. Connecting with more people creates more opportunities for serendipity.

In the section on implications for businesses, I'll give examples of businesses of all sizes and restrictions doing well in social networks, and how they're doing it. Keep the following term in mind as you explore social networks and prime yourself to understand the implications in your own business: *digital kinesthesia.*

Kinesthesia is that physical sense of your body in space—the knowledge of the location of your hand even though your eyes may be closed so you can't see it. Digital kinesthesia is the sense of your being in the ether of the online world, and how you interact in that world—how the physical, emotional, psychological, and intellectual aspects of self are stimulated and engaged in the digital realm. It is the online version of your senses, as well as the linchpin to how commerce is taking place, and how it will evolve. A simple example is the agitation you might feel when you haven't been on e-mail for a while and you know that more and more messages are backing up. A more complex sense is in knowing how your friends or colleagues are collectively engaging around an idea or opportunity.

Your Employees and Business Partners in Social Networks

I said earlier that you should join a social network; in addition, you should join a business network. And yes, download the app for that business network on your smartphone if you don't have one already.

And, yes, download the app for that social network on your smartphone. Try a professional's networking site (there are a few). The rapid growth of these sites is a key sociological indicator of how seriously people are taking social networks. See how many of your employees, colleagues, and friends are on these networks. Depending on the industry you work in and the company you keep, it could already be most of them. A generation ago this would have been seen as trouble; employees out looking for a job. But today it is standard, and you need to grasp and accept that. They aren't there looking for a job—they are connecting with opportunities of all kinds. Partnerships, sales leads, product ideas . . . if you accept the power of these networks, there is a chance you can leverage the phenomenon instead of being threatened by it. Openness is the most important prescription for business in the social mobile cloud.

Every person is now the CEO of himself or herself. Every person is his or her own brand. In Chapters 8 and 9, I will go into much greater detail about the shifting nature of relationships between employees and employer. But for now, in terms of social networking technology itself, it is important to bear in mind that people are creating their own empire, their own strategy, their own social network for fostering new business relationships and conducting present business. As an employer, you want the best and brightest to be interested in interacting with your business, participating in projects and on teams. To that end, a professional social network can serve as banner advertising for your company, as well as a scouting ground.

Searching and understanding these social networking sites is a quintessential example of how much our old thinking needs to change. The number one paradigm shift in thinking that needs to take place is to stop hoarding and start sharing. If a star employee having a presence on a professional networking site threatens you, you aren't thinking it through in a social mobile cloud manner. First of all, contained within any employee profile is your company name, front and center, a little free advertising for you. If the employee is a particularly good one, this reflects very well on you. Perhaps with a little encouragement, a happy employee will recruit people to work at your company.

This leads to perhaps the single most important aspect of employees engaging in social networks: Every single employee is now a spokesperson for your company. And they're not just chatting at a cocktail party; the whole world can hear. Keep this in mind as you develop your social mobile cloud strategy. Every organization will need policies about behavior online. You certainly want to encourage positive messages. Any attempt to curb any conversation would be like a Third World dictator trying to stop people from using the Internet in order to maintain a control that has already been lost. And most organizations don't have the unpleasant option of rolling tanks into the public squares and positioning snipers on the rooftops. So just make sure everyone understands the implications. For instance, if you own a vodka company, you would prefer that your employees don't show off drunken pictures of themselves on a social network, but some might and those employees need to understand the consequences for the company and themselves.

This sort of policy setting and enforcement is a tricky subject and will require guidance in the area of privacy. What rights do you have to tell employees how to behave on their social networks? I'll go into this area in detail in Chapter 14. There is no set answer, and you will need to deal with this issue in terms of the culture of your company. The phrase to keep in mind as you set policy is due diligence: due diligence on information. Don't be secretive, just careful. Inaccuracies, untruths, or incomplete information can ruin credibility quickly online.

One social network technology trend to watch—and this one is more in terms of your supply chain—is secure social networks. For larger organizations that need to utilize social networks to communicate within their supply chains, it is essential to make sure there is encryption and robust data mining capability. They are on the way and businesses absolutely need to experiment with these technologies in the ADAPT process. Makers of salesforce automation software have recognized that their products are fundamentally about social networking. What could your company accomplish if your salespeople behaved more collaboratively? What improvements in the quality of customer service would emerge if the best talents of all your employees could be shared all the time?

I hope you've gotten the message in this chapter that—it is not just about social media, or social networking, or even co-creation. Think about your business as becoming a social enterprise where every function, every process, has been transformed by people working more effectively together.

CHAPTER

3

Mobile

The Great Untethering

The smartphone remote control is of course the key to great untethering—the disconnection of our ability to work from a need to be at a particular fixed location. And no longer attached to our desks to get work done, we can now go down to the factory floor or out to dinner but stay connected to some critical business event that may be unfolding elsewhere. The capabilities of the average portable computing device are moving at the exponential pace of Moore's Law—processor speed, memory, network connections, all are doubling and doubling again and will continue to do so. And the role that it plays in extending our human capabilities into the superhuman is forever changing our expectations and behaviors.

There are three critical areas we will examine—the most obvious is the always-on connectivity, from which arises a new state of *persistent digital engagement*. But equally as important is the role our mobile computers are playing in helping us to make sense of the world—augmented or annotated reality applications that superimpose information over our physical surroundings add a sixth sense to the existing senses that we have previously relied on to navigate our physical environment. Increasingly sophisticated electronics in devices (and in the future, implants) are substantially extending our standard five senses in distance, sensitivity, and (through the cloud) ability to understand what we are sensing and even share it with others as we have the experience.

Before we examine how these three trends of connectivity, augmented reality, and sophisticated sensors are extending our capabilities and transforming how we work, a quick history and overview of the technical capabilities of our new pocket computers is in order.

The New Technical Capabilities

Mobile telephony is at least in one sense 80 years old. In the 1930s, a passenger on certain ocean liners could place a call via radio to the still new landline network of telephones. But amazingly, by the second half of the 1940s, companies had introduced car phones to a few cities in the United States even though the necessary equipment weighed about 80 pounds. The pace of innovation in this market was dominated by Moore's Law—the doubling of computational power over time—such that it wasn't until 1973 that the first handheld mobile phone was demonstrated. The first prototype device still weighed 2.5 pounds, although accelerating miniaturization quickly began to shrink the size and weight of these handheld phones.

In parallel to the development of smaller and smaller phones, another industry was developing a handheld technology—computer manufacturers, which had just begun in the 1970s to make a personal computer, also embarked on the journey to build a portable computer. While the first computers that could be easily moved from place to place were demonstrated in the 1970s, the early 1980s saw an explosion of commercial offerings. Often weighing in at as much as 20 pounds, however, these devices were often derided as "luggable" computers, indicating how much work it took to move them from place to place.

In order to bring computing into a handheld format, designers looked to limit the capabilities of these devices and a new computing category called personal digital assistants (PDAs) was created. These devices were focused on replacing paper for keeping track of our appointments and contacts as well as performing a limited number of tasks. The idea was novel—people would want to carry a computer around everywhere they went. Both industries, companies making personal computers and the ones making mobile phones, saw an opportunity in this new category of ubiquitous computing although they approached the opportunity in different ways.

In hindsight, it seems obvious that computing and mobile phones would eventually merge. Companies that had leadership positions in the manufacturing and distribution of phones were early leaders in portable computing as well. Several phone manufacturers developed products to provide the same limited capabilities of the PDA (appointments, address book) in the phone. In the case of phone numbers in the address book, there was of course a direct value to making calls, the primary function of the mobile phone. But initially combining a PDA with a phone had limited appeal—for those people who would have carried both, there was now just one device to carry. But adoption of a much more expensive phone just to avoid carrying a paper appointment book hardly made sense to the majority of mobile phone buyers.

A number of manufacturers experimented with adding other kinds of features into a mobile phone. One of the first such experiments was a phone with a digital camera. Several different markets emerged—music phones, camera phones, and a gaming system in a phone. But while all of this innovation was taking place in the mobile phone market, the personal computer industry was readying a response.

The computer industry delivered three major innovations to the mobile phone market—a great mobile Web browsing experience, a touch screen interface, and a new way of selling and activating phones that did not depend on carriers. And by providing a system for allowing third parties to write apps for phones, the computing industry extended its lead over the mobile phone industry.

As market share has dwindled for traditional mobile phone makers, many have exited the market. While a few noncomputing industry players are still in the market, many of them have now partnered with computing industry players for the operating system and access to third-party apps. The industry has largely concluded the battle for the mobile device and firmly established that it will be a handheld computer that can make calls and not a phone that has a few computing features that will succeed in the marketplace.

In five short years, an entire industry was transformed by the ability to embed computing into that industry's products. And our expectations as consumers have changed rapidly. In 2010, only 19 percent of the U.S. population used a smartphone. But today that number is more than 50 percent, and if people over the age of 55 are removed from the calculation, the number is over 75 percent.

Connectivity

What can you do today that you couldn't imagine having done five years ago? In every instance and with increasing ease, the cloud is just a few screen touches away, delivering news, information, opinion, connections, and the ability to take action with other people—changing what we are capable of knowing and doing. We are entering the era of persistent digital engagement when our mobile devices allow us to maintain an online connection to friends and colleagues from the moment we wake up to the moment we go to sleep, only intermittently interrupted by in-person interactions, physical activity, travel, or other personal activities (and sometimes not even then).

These expectations of connectivity to information and people from our mobile phones are beginning to extend to other products that we use. From viewing the charging status in an electric car to accessing a home security system or tracking how far and fast we run using sensors in running shoes, mobile phones are now connecting us to everything in our lives—our cars, our homes, and all of the products we use. The design possibilities for every company's products and services must be reexamined by the opportunity to embed sensors, computing, and wireless connectivity and the ability to extend persistent digital engagement and to transform our experience of those products and services.

Being in a state of persistent digital engagement means that friends, colleagues, information, and access to processes and systems have become an extension of everyday existence. Social gives us the network of people to engage with, but mobile makes it possible to engage whenever and wherever—which in practice means everywhere and all the time.

From complex tasks like worker communication to smaller personal tasks like getting to a meeting on time without getting caught in traffic, the smartphone remote control handles the request. Remember the days when you planned ahead, examining the path you would take on highways or public transportation to arrive at your destination? Now you don't even need to know the address you are heading toward to get there on time. Get close, search the Web for the business or landmark you are headed toward, and the cloud will deliver to your handheld device the optimal path to your destination, current traffic conditions, and bus schedules included. Making plans to meet friends? No need to plan ahead as mobile allows ad hoc coordination, resolving a specific meeting spot at the last minute.

Accessing information about the restaurants nearby, finding a gas station, navigating a transit system—every one of these tasks is made easier with a mobile device that connects to people and data rich Internet sites either through the Web browser or through specialized applications that make searching and using information even easier.

Perhaps you are having a discussion with a colleague, dependent on a specific piece of data or an answer from a third colleague not in the room. There is no longer the need to have the conversation halt and continue only after getting the critical information. With just a few taps on your smartphone, the information comes to life. Or if the question is for a colleague who isn't in the room, or in the building, or even on the continent, a quick message during the meeting to the person's handheld device and an answer back again keeps things moving ahead instead of stalling until he or she happens to be able to take a call or is on e-mail or is back in the office.

Mobility is almost as essential to the new productivity equation as social—reducing the cost of coordination is in part about reducing cycle time, which is about both expanding the possible number of people that can answer a question (social) and about increasing the likelihood that the right person is available to answer (mobility). Social and mobile working together smash down barriers to productivity, promote peer communication, and break down hierarchical and organizational walls that companies developed to efficiently manage communications in a connectivity-poor world.

We are just at the beginning stages of understanding how the combination of powerful information services in the cloud accessed by always on, always connected devices will have a profound effect on how we live and work. We are in the first years of the great untethering. While we have had incredible access to information from our desks for a decade, only in the last five years has that information been in our pockets, available as an immediate extension of our memory, our knowledge, and our ability to comprehend complex environments. Untethering means easy access to information and people on every level of work and life. It changes how we work, where we work, when we work, and even the work itself.

Here are a few examples of work redefined by mobility:

- An airline employee no longer tethered to a check-in counter but instead able to solve any passenger problem anywhere in the airport through a connected mobile device.

- A manufacturing employee able to snap a photo of a hazardous condition or a potential manufacturing defect and instantly transmit that photo to the members of a supervisory review group, who in turn are instantly receiving the photo on their mobile devices and can discuss online what action to take.
- A quick service restaurant where employees make food and deliver it to a customer's table, but they never take an order and customers never wait in line because all of the ordering is done through a smartphone.
- Retail stores with no cash registers and no lines because every employee has a mobile device that can process the customer order and accept payment so employees can come to the customers at the time of purchase rather than vice versa.
- A construction worker who can view exactly how the specific part of the building should be assembled by viewing the plans on a mobile device, overlayed visually on the partially constructed building, and perhaps even tracking the progress against plan and flagging in real time when errors are being made.

Each of these scenarios is already coming to life somewhere in the world, and if your company isn't thinking about how work will change in your business, you are already falling behind.

Reality Redefined: The Physical World with Data Overlay

You can now purchase a brilliant application that allows you to "see" a sign in Spanish rewritten automatically into English. This is not just a translation of the Spanish on the sign into English, but the sign itself, viewed through the smartphone camera, rewritten. If it is a yellow sign with black Helvetica script in Spanish, on your cell phone screen you will see the same yellow sign with black Helvetica script in English. This capability to take information from our local environment, combine it with intelligence in a computer somewhere else in the world, and create an entirely new composite reality will change everything about how we interact with the people, places, and things around us.

One can even envision a time in the not-so-distant future when a young person who has grown up with augmented or annotated reality (as this composite reality is sometimes called) will feel afraid and alone when the information overlay on the physical world is for some reason missing. What we think of as reality will increasingly be a combination of what we see with our eyes and what we see with our machines.

The construction worker in the previous example could view his building through a construction lens and see exactly how the next part of the building needed to come together. An airline employee could look through a special lens at an aircraft or a baggage cart and see information about that particular flight or the intended destination of those bags, overlaid on the real world objects. An engineer could view a bridge with embedded wireless sensors and watch in real time the stress in different parts of the structure as vehicles passed over.

It is important to recognize that mobility won't just change how we connect to the people and information available on the Internet but also how it will change our connection to everything in our physical world as well as how those objects are connected and how the interface for sensing those connections matures, changing how we see and hear everything around us.

Life Streaming: Access to a Photographic Memory

Portable cameras connected to data networks—mobile video—is changing how we interact with our environments and each other. One experimenter in this new technology, a 20-something young man, wore a video camera connected to a wireless data device, and his fans talked with one another in an online forum about what he was doing (or what he should do). Every second of his life, every conversation he had, every place he went was recorded permanently and could be searched and reviewed at his leisure. What did that person say to me? How did that argument go? Where was it that I parked the car? With a permanent and complete recording of our lives, we could compensate for the fallibility of our own memory of events.

Beyond how this technology changes our own personal memory, attaching cameras to patrol cars, or even directly to police officers and soldiers, is already becoming an important part of how we create a safer world. A police officer's behavior changes when he or she knows that everything is being recorded for others to see.

In the 1990s, with increasing lawsuits against state and highway patrol agencies for race-based traffic stops, police departments deployed in-car camera systems to record an unbiased account of each incident. In a 2002 study of the impact of these systems, officers reported that they used the tapes extensively as a means of self-critique. In addition, officers reported that when they informed citizens that the traffic stop was being recorded, it also helped to calm confrontations.

Recorded memory is a great mediator. Just the knowledge that a record of an interaction is being made can change a private interaction into a public interaction and significantly shift the behavior of the participants. There are things that people will say and do if they think that these actions or words can later be plausibly denied. Although recordings can be modified, the knowledge that a recording is being made can improve our interactions.

Recorded memories give you as close to an objective view of yourself as possible, which translates into improved work and personal relationships. Your memory, in effect, has an added dimension. There may be no pure sense of objectivity, but storing memory for later access will certainly add perspective to your subjectivity. Think of any photo of yourself from long ago. Right after that photo was taken, you might have had a certain opinion of it. Twenty years later, you will likely have a very different opinion of it. Ask a 40-year-old to look at a photo of himself when he was 20. Even if he didn't like the photo when he was 20, chances are at age 40 that his first reaction will be positive: "Look how young I was!"

Temporal perspective, the wisdom that the passing of time and accumulated life experience gives you, can add richness to your thinking and your decision making. That is not to say that you need a recording of your episodic memory to think well, but it does give credence to the premise that stored, shared memory has value on many levels, and there is no reason to resist it. Take advantage of it, starting with getting as pervasively computational as possible at any given time.

Cyborg

Memory, knowledge acquisition, data visualization, decision making, and the creation of social and business bonds—an enormous part of what we do with our brains—is now being mediated and extended by our mobile devices. In the 1960s, the word *cyborg* was coined from the combination of cybernetics (a 1940s word for the science of communication systems) and organism. Cyborg was defined then (here from the *New Oxford American Dictionary*, and in some dictionaries still) as: "a fictional or hypothetical person whose physical abilities are extended beyond normal human limitations by mechanical elements built into the body."

But extending our physical abilities is no longer fictional or hypothetical. By tapping into information systems with our mobile devices, we are extending our capacity to function. We are now entering an age in which people without such a device (or a business that fails to provide for them) will be at a distinct competitive disadvantage from those who do have and use them.

The mobile device is at once a sensor and a portal—letting us both detect conditions in the local environment around us and connect with global information and people to make sense of what we are seeing and hearing. How this will impact your business depends on what you do to make use of these capabilities. What capabilities will you put into the hands of your customers to enable them to interact more easily with your business? How will you support your employees with real-time information and analytical tools?

BYOD and the Consumerization of IT

The tools that we use to access information are becoming a part of how we define ourselves. As an extension of our abilities, we feel incomplete without them. And so why, when we get to work, would we want to be without the mobile device that we have when we are away from work? Especially when the definition of when we are at work is itself in flux.

We are facing the twin challenge of enterprises that must mobilize their workforces but workers who show up with their device of choice already in their hands. Unthinkable for most businesses in the age of the PC, suddenly the idea that a worker might be allowed to "bring your own device" (BYOD) is gaining credibility in even the largest companies.

But this didn't come about because IT departments thought it was a good idea. But rather, employees equipped with more and more powerful technology in their personal lives simply started bringing that technology with them into the office and expecting that they could work outside the office using these devices. Although you can threaten to fire one or two employees for breaking the rules, companies quickly reached a tipping point where most employees—including some of the most senior ones—are no longer satisfied with the technology issued by the IT department and ask, "Why can't I do my work with what I already use at home?"

Ubiquitous and powerful consumer technology has given employees the ability to question the CIO—even offer compelling alternatives to what had previously been a superior technological resource within the internal IT organization.

4

Plug Yourself into the Cloud

Social networks are expanding exponentially, everyone is dispersed and mobile, armed with remote control smartphones and acting as CEO of their personal brand that must be marketed online. It leads to this phenomenon: We are collectively plugging into the new digital workplace of the twenty-first century . . . the cloud.

The name *cloud* itself suggests exalted and open status, and the cloud certainly does take our lives, our relationships, and our collaboration to a new level. But what is this cloud anyway?

After a long period of design divergence, large-scale computing is collapsing into a small set of accepted standards. And just like the electrical grid, standardization is driving down cost, increasing accessibility, and—in making complexity disappear—allowing us to plug in to computing as easily as we might plug in to a power outlet.

Four Key Technologies

Four key technologies are being standardized—servers, networks, data storage, and software. Companies are increasingly building their data centers in exactly the same way that every other company does including companies dedicated to providing Internet services. There is a dominant design that has emerged in data centers.

With servers, it's the x86 architecture that has won, pushing all manner of other servers out of the way. Where once the data center had an array of different shapes and colors, now it is filled with rack after rack of entirely interchangeable parts.

The network has standardized on TCP/IP—the protocol of the Internet. For some people it is difficult to imagine that anything else ever existed. Token ring? DECnet? Most readers of this book would have to look those terms up on a search engine to discover that they were once important networking standards.

Intelligent storage on solid-state devices is increasing in capacity as quickly as the massive quantities of data we are creating grow. Without the spinning disks and other moving parts, these storage devices are reliable and can be organized to place data close to where it will be used.

And finally in software, the service-oriented-architecture for applications using application programming interfaces (APIs) has created a standard way to build loosely coupled applications that can be accessed by any device.

So go a step further than just joining a social network. Whip out your new smartphone and create your personal cloud. Sign up for one of the new cloud services. Similar to the concept of understanding social networks in Chapter 2, there is nothing like understanding the cloud by participating on a personal level.

However, the essential definition of cloud computing from a business leader's perspective is this simple and compelling picture to bear in mind as you sign up for your personal cloud: a limitless offsite infrastructure connecting you to everything and everyone.

How the cloud works is that all data and applications pertinent to your business are accessible by a public network, a grid. Remember, it is like the way electricity works: You have no idea where the network resides, or what equipment makes up that network, and you don't care. You don't pay for hardware and you don't worry about anything.

Now also incorporate the definition of the cloud from a marketer's perspective: It is the infrastructure from which to develop deep relationships with customers. You have already figured that out from joining social networks. When we are in that new state of persistent digital engagement, the place our digital selves reside is in the cloud. And the cloud is collecting data about everything we do and say while we are there. The point of saying it from the cloud computing perspective is to reiterate that the triumvirate is inseparable: social mobile cloud.

As it stands technologically, we are in the nascent stages of virtualizing our infrastructure. What that means in practical terms is to allow the vision for what your company will do in the cloud to be bigger than the present infrastructure. Don't clip the wings of your social mobile cloud team. The rate at which the infrastructure will develop is exponentially greater than ever before.

The point is to not hold back on business development visions employing the cloud when you engage in your ADAPT program. By the time you build it out, the cloud and your employees will be ready. Understanding how you can use the cloud as an extension of your product or service is key to embracing digital transformation and how it will make you and your business more competitive.

The mobile application Word Lens that I described in Chapter 3 is an interesting example of this scenario. Having a way to look up the meaning of a foreign word is essential for a traveler and a mobile dictionary is only a little more useful than a paper one. But an app that allows you to look at the screen of your smartphone, with the camera aimed at a sign in Spanish, and instantly see the same sign in English transforms our experience of the world. The cloud is leveraged to process the language conversion and the mobile phone makes it easy for us to consume this computation and put it to use.

Online translation is doing the same thing for spoken language. Record someone speaking in French (or dozens of languages) and with the right app a written text translation can appear on the screen of your smartphone. Or push a button and have it speak the phrase back to you in your own language. These apps work because they can connect to the cloud where the translation really happens.

Cloud computing combined with a mobile device can change reality (or at least the way we perceive reality).

Benefits of the Cloud Are Heavenly for Business

Key immediate benefits of the cloud are working more closely with trading partners and making better decisions. There are simply more options for sharing information, both in terms of retrieving and disseminating data, and for the workgroups with access to the data. It is again all about connection, and the cloud is the place where it happens.

Businesses are standardizing on computing infrastructure and software architecture. The ease and speed with which data is shared is the real hat trick here. Publish data through an API and your trading party can incorporate those data into its business processes.

Often being able to make the optimal decision in a supply chain is dependent on access to real-time information. So far, in larger organizations, even the ones with multimillion-dollar analytics-driven, data mining software solutions with BI front ends, real-time information about business processes is elusive, in part because the inputs haven't been available and in part because it is lacking a human component.

Once the data are available, your ability to retrieve deeply tucked in, cross-referenced data and the ability to deliver it quickly will mean a serious competitive advantage. And don't just think business to business. There was more data stored online in 2010 than in the entire aggregated history of the Internet. Consumers are filling databases of information about themselves at record speed. You can find out anything you want to know with the right data mining strategy. And in terms of technology interface, dashboards are vital because you need more than information; you need a highly navigable way of looking at information. The term dashboard is exactly what it sounds like: your screen is real-time visibility into your business.

A tip to remember when looking at data mining tools: If you see the term *dashboard* without the term *analytics-driven* attached to it, then the solution isn't more than a bunch of pretty pictures. And without a real-time aspect at this point, don't bother with it. The bar has been raised.

I will get to examples of real-time data-driven decision making and the importance of systems thinking in Chapter 15 and Chapter 16. There are also valuable examples of data-driven decision making that are not real time, but let's just say that in the social mobile cloud arena the faster you get the data, the better off you are. Think of the concept of serendipity I touched on before: being in the right place at the right time and capitalizing on naturally occurring trends on the fly.

You need a real-time dashboard to leverage serendipity. For example, on a social network, people are suddenly talking about airline flight cancellations due to snowstorms and needing to make alternate plans. If you sell lodging, alternate transportation, car rentals and such, you could seize the moment and quickly offer a captive needy marketplace discounts, special offers, or full travel packages. You would attract customers you otherwise would not have.

Drawbacks of the Cloud—Just Like Any Grid

There is so much that is compelling about the cloud, but you cannot properly develop a strategy without understanding the drawbacks.

However, some of the drawbacks are also potential inspiration for opportunities.

The number one drawback, which is not conducive to any activity whatsoever, is that when your data are in the cloud, you can only work when there is network connectivity: high speed and always-on network connectivity. It's like the electricity grid, where there is no light without power. So you create a new dependency within your business. But that said, for many kinds of work in the enterprise today, that is already a requirement.

There are companies with network architectures that are already addressing this problem. You can place a server in a remote office that caches data so employees can continue working even with slow or intermittent Internet connectivity— just as a battery stores energy for use when electricity is unavailable or unreliable.

By the way, in terms of social mobile cloud being an entwined concept, this goes for all aspects, include data backup. Mobile, tablets, and eventually all of your access devices are just windows into the cloud. You may need to sync up and take key data with you when you aren't connected, but much of the time you will simply depend on ubiquitous Internet access. But by deciding which data to take with you when you are going to be without Internet access for intervals, such as on an ill-equipped airplane that lacks Internet connectivity, you focus and prioritize your work. Instead of taking everything, you take what needs to get done immediately.

Leveling the Playing Field

Earlier, I talked about leveling the playing field. Cloud computing among small business owners is linked hand in hand to the rise of mobile computing. Small business owners and employees alike must be nimble, often working more flexible hours than their larger counterparts, needing access to data from home and work and while in constant transit, at all times of day and night.

But the entire workforce is increasingly behaving like small business owners and employees, because of the nature of the market-place and a trend I call *fractalization*. I'll delve more deeply into that employee-employer relationship shift issue in Chapter 9. But first, it is important to grasp the relationship of business to mobile technology, literally the new tools of your trade.

Think of a salesperson at lunch with a potential client. The client asks a question, essentially raising an objection to your product or service offering. In the bad days before the cloud, the salesperson would be forced to jot down the question and say, "I'll get back to you." Then there would be three more days of phone tag until the salesperson can get back in touch, and in the end you lose a week in the sales process.

But now, with a live chat app on your smartphone, you can have the answer to the question, and you keep the sales process in the moment. With the right answers spontaneously in the middle of the conversation, you can get the client excited. Remember the idea of gamification. Even answering questions can become a game with the right app. Think about how you might reward members of your team for digitally leaping to the assistance of their colleagues. And this is not just a sales game for you. People love trivia and data answers of all kinds, and potential clients are no exception. When the salesperson and the client are both enjoying the game of making a deal, that deal will close faster. Certainly, clients sometimes stall as a matter of course or of habit. But the game of a collaborative social networking app pushes past these old habits and enables salespeople to close deals during lunches.

Plug Yourself into the Cloud

The capabilities of the cloud will change how you work and how your business works. If you are a business at the scale to own your data centers, you may elect to realign your physical systems' architecture to look like that of public cloud providers. If you are a smaller business, you may give up altogether on having your own systems and just depend entirely on the public cloud. The important lesson is that the opportunities for competitive advantage are shifting. The IT department is not going to provide the enterprise with an advantage through running information systems more cost effectively. And to the contrary, the IT department may hold back your business when you could be getting a greater advantage by adopting public cloud services and the new innovations they bring.

Now is the time to reexamine the role of IT and the CIO—recognizing that simultaneously IT is become substantially more critical to all business processes while also becoming more accessible and comprehensible to all business users. This is not a contradiction but a complementary phenomenon—IT is going mainstream. And the cloud is the place it is happening.

PART

II

How Business Will Be Changed by the Social Mobile Cloud

CHAPTER

ADAPT

Adapting to Change

A number of times in the first few chapters of this book, I have mentioned the need to learn how to ADAPT to change. In outlining the disruptive technologies of the social mobile cloud that are simultaneously arriving at our doorsteps, I provided a glimpse into the forcing function for change. However, technology is only 20 percent of what is happening, the rest is about people and their behaviors and organizations and their processes. And to survive and thrive in the new world that technology is bringing us, we will need to learn to ADAPT—both as individuals and as organizations.

Technological Changes

Throughout history, technology has brought change to the way we live and work and required that we adapt to these changes. For most of the history of civilization, this need to adapt occurred over generations with the occasional turning point event that accelerated change—what a geologist would refer to as cataclysmic change or in evolutionary biology as punctuated equilibrium. Many of those moments of punctuation in civilization were brought about by technological changes.

The invention of the printing press was one such change; bringing with it the ability to eliminate the tedious task of hand reproduction of texts. But it also democratized access to information and had unanticipated consequences for both the church and governments. Even before this change, the rapid evolution of siege weapons transformed warfare and by extension architecture (castles ceased to make much sense as a reliable defense against invaders). History is littered with these changes and the massive impacts that they can have on society and its institutions.

But in the past century, the pace of technological change has accelerated to the point where we must anticipate radical shifts within our lifetimes—not just once or twice but many times. It is no longer just a king or the pope that must wrestle with the implications and adjust policies and strategies. Now we must all learn to ADAPT to change and our new state demands that our method of adaptation accounts for change that will be continuous. We must embrace a new way of thinking about change and how we change ourselves (and our organizations) to thrive on these changes.

A starting point is to understand how we cope with change of any kind. The ADAPT model is a five-stage process by which new technologies can be understood and ultimately absorbed by individuals and companies. This process itself is a type of game, with a goal in mind, challenges at each turn, and rewards for persistence and smart decisions. The global economy and information technology has steadily increased the pace at which the best companies move through these phases, which creates an imperative for you to understand and absorb new innovations. The five stages are:

1. **Awareness.** There is a first moment when you (and your organization) become aware of a new technology and its potential to change how you live or work. For example, in the early 1990s, businesses all began to notice this new technology called the Internet. However, because it is hard to know when a given change is "real" (will have a lasting important impact) versus a passing fad (of which we have seen many in our careers), there is a tendency to initially respond with:
2. **Denial.** Organizations have a natural inclination to reject change, sometimes referred to as organizational antibodies, although we can feel this resistance in ourselves as well and not just as a collective rejection of change. By the mid-1990s, many reasonable and experienced people thought that the Internet was a fad, certain to be pushed aside by a more orderly media experience (the information superhighway). The initial test of

an individual and an organization is the speed with which a knee-jerk reaction to deny change can be pushed aside in order to move on to:

3. **Acceptance.** The first stage of showing true adaptability is the willingness to accept change. Understanding the change, evaluating the importance and the implications, can come later. However, the initial denial and rejection must give way to a willingness to explore and to understand a new technology and the changes it might bring. Embracing the idea of gamification, and being a gamer, will help here. Playful people are great explorers. At first, this may be limited to rethinking existing processes and simply reimplementing them by using new tools. In the beginning days of the Internet, a common first step online for retailers, for example, was simply to put their product catalog onto the Web. This brought some small advantages (reaching customers without printing expensive catalogs), but without rethinking those processes the advantage remained limited. The next test of adaptability requires that you make:

4. **Progress.** The new technology adds new capabilities to the organization and the initial reimplementation of existing processes creates incremental benefits. From these new capabilities there should come recognition that something different can be achieved because of these capabilities. A measure of organizational adaptability is whether this happens through intentional reengineering or through the more organic process of people shifting their own behaviors to work around aspects of the old processes. For example, Internet retailers had a choice of providing a function to allow user reviews of products, something never before possible with printed catalogs. But where companies were slow to see this new use, customers began to write their own reviews in other places. Over time, these reviews became a more fruitful starting place for a potential customer to research their purchase, siphoning business away from retailers who failed to offer this feature. Those companies that continue down the path of adaptation though are ready for the next stage of:

5. **Transformation.** Finally, a rethinking of business processes in the context of the new technology and an exploration of possibilities beyond those processes can result in entirely

new products, services, or ways of working. In this last stage, there is a realization that the technology provides a new context in which to consider an organization's challenges, enabling ways of working that may not have been possible before the advent of these new capabilities. For retailers, as an example, the ability to allow customers to use websites to entirely customize products has led to the development of new on-demand and custom manufacturing businesses with much better margins and higher loyalty than traditional undifferentiated product sales.

The ADAPT process is not limited to just the business world as in the previous example. You can find examples in your own life and in many other kinds of organizations in our society: education, government, charities, etc. Human beings are "wired" for developing what we call expertise. We learn how to react to our environment, and as long as the environment stays the same, we get better and better at reacting.

But we also need to develop the ability to question whether our environment has changed—and whether we need to unlearn some of those reactions. We must develop the ability to ask whether our reactions are protecting us or creating a new danger by making us inflexible to properly adapt to new conditions.

At the Core of Today's Change: Transaction Cost Economics

What do all the technologies described in Part I have in common? They transform the cost of transactions. Each of the technologies in the social mobile cloud reduces the cost of communication and coordination—the two largest components in the cost of doing business. Everything we do in business is governed by transaction costs. Innovation, production, sales and marketing, distribution, exchange, consumption, support—every process requires people to interact with one another to get work done. We have had to organize these interactions very carefully to limit communication because it has been so expensive. But the environment changed and what was expensive is now cheap.

The first lesson in learning how to ADAPT is to develop skills for asking the right questions. In this example, if all you do when transaction costs drop is revel in the fact that you can reduce the cost of running the same processes in the same ways, then you've missed the necessary adaptation. When employees become untethered, when networks of people inside and outside your company are solving problems together, it is time to rethink the processes altogether. This is the transformation stage that adaptation ultimately leads to if done well. In the second part of this book, I will examine a series of ways in which our business processes need to be rethought for the world of the social mobile cloud.

In addition to learning how to ask good questions, what are the skills we need to ADAPT? Start with curiosity, openness, a thick skin, and willingness to be wrong. Learning from failure, rather than being afraid to fail. And a constant willingness to learn—a predisposition to experimentation. Ask yourself: Where are you holding back right now? Not experimenting with something that you could learn from? Do you have a smartphone? Are you on a social network? Are you engaging in the easy things to experiment with? If not, how will you be able to move on to the more difficult things?

In Chapters 6, 7, and 8, I will explore how the environment for doing business is changing, and how you will be challenged to ADAPT personally and professionally to these changes. The first change is in the way we behave as individual customers—how the combination of the social mobile cloud has created a new state of persistent digital engagement that is changing our expectations as consumers of products and services. We want the companies we do business with to be available, responsive, honest, and transparent. We expect that the information we want is available when and where we want it. And when we are ready to purchase, we want to do so with as little friction and as little effort as possible.

The second shift is around how technology is increasingly embedded in the things we purchase and the services we use—changing (and enhancing) our experience of what we buy. Companies are now adding connected information services to everything they sell, often redefining the products as services in themselves. Running shoes, home alarm systems, and electric cars are three examples where the smartphone has become a remote control for collecting and analyzing data and controlling objects. Companies will have to rethink their value propositions and often business models as "software eats the world."

Finally, I will explore how the reduced cost of communication and of coordination is fundamentally changing how we make decisions, develop products, and solve other problems in our organizations. Crowd storming, crowd sourcing, collaboration, and co-creation are all facets of a new capacity for organizations to link up their employees, break through organizational walls and connect with trading partners, and even to make customers and prospects part of smarter processes for solving problems.

CHAPTER 6

Persistent Digital Engagement

The New Digital Consumer

On a recent Saturday morning, I was sitting in a café and heard a great song from a band I didn't recognize. I asked the staff and they told me the name of the band. Before I had finished my latte, I had purchased the album and downloaded it to my smartphone. Later that day, I read a great article in a national newspaper (online, of course) and mentioned it on a social network. Within five minutes, I had received responses from two friends—one in the Bay Area and one in Finland.

Perhaps you have had similar experiences. Always-on Internet access through your mobile phone allowing you to instantly learn or buy something. Social networks providing connectivity to friends and family near and far. These social networks and Internet connected smartphones are coming together to define the new consumer condition: persistent digital engagement.

A number of thinkers in the middle part of the last century foresaw this new state although they didn't anticipate how the Internet and smartphones would become the pivotal technologies to bring this vision to life. In the 1950s, there was a rush to understand the (then new) medium of television through the still-fresh experience of a pre–mass media marketplace. Television was seen as taking the neighborhood conversation in the local post office and extending it to every post office in every corner of the world—bringing the natural human way of two-way and tribal interaction to a global audience no longer limited by time or distance.

But the technology defined a one-way mass audience broadcast model that the television industry embraced, and it never delivered the neighborhood conversation (a small exception would be community access channels). What was lost in the broadcast model was the ability to talk back—the two-way interaction that was the key to the post office conversation going global.

Finally, beginning in the last part of the twentieth century, online services and then the Internet began to realize the global community vision. Over the past 25 years, we have with ever-increasing speed and scale absorbed and embraced a two-way mass communication medium that is now overwhelming and replacing broadcast as the way we understand and engage with the world around us. Among younger people, this transition has already occurred, and the Internet, increasingly mobile, dominates their leisure time. And not just to consume media (although that is certainly a part of the mix) but to also engage and interact with people. Just like the village post office going global.

A new consumer reality is emerging, defined by a constant online presence connecting consumers to information and each other. At an accelerating pace, consumer expectations are changing—consumers expecting easy access to information and opinion and the ability to interact instantly with friends and families. They are taking this new persistent digital engagement into every part of their lives, especially when they are considering purchases. Consumers are online all the time, and they want the companies they buy from to be there too, and to be responsive, interactive, and trustworthy.

Some companies look at this new globally connected consumer and wonder whether there is a role for them in these online spaces. Do consumers want to hear from companies or only from one another?

But the fact that consumers are primarily talking among themselves doesn't mean that companies lack opportunities to participate in these online conversations. On the contrary, the need to create and maintain social and mobile experiences to address the new consumer state of persistent digital engagement will require that companies develop fluency in digital product development, social technologies, and create collaboration across groups that have often worked in isolation. While a complete transformation would involve significant investment, here are a few areas where companies can begin adjusting their strategies.

Customer Service Is the New Marketing

A starting point for companies wondering how they should engage with consumers is to look at how customer service can be a part of their marketing presence. A first place to look is at consumers who have abandoned a transaction or not made an intended purchase because of poor customer service—many will try a new brand or company for a better service experience. As part of a shift in customer expectations brought about by the Internet, consumers increasingly demand great customer service online and they expect answers to their questions within 24 hours. And if ignored by brands in social media and social networking, consumers can now loudly (and visibly) complain to others.

How a company chooses to project its brand values by engaging with customers online to solve their problems or simply answer their questions can tell others a lot about the company's customer service commitment. And from this commitment, potential buyers will make inferences about the quality of a company's products or services. Integrating social streams into existing customer service workflows is part of the solution, but the skill set for engaging directly with consumers in a public forum is different from the usual one-on-one customer service process and will require additional training. Also, some questions will arise that exceed the normal set of issues addressed by customer service. Linking different groups beyond customer service together—including communications, marketing, sales, and even product development—will be essential to creating a successful social customer support presence online.

Connecting Digitally at the Physical Point of Sale

The fact that consumers now have mobile Internet access in their hands at the point of sale means that often buyers will know more than sellers about a given transaction—an important reversal of the asynchronous market information that has been the norm throughout the history of mass markets. Nevertheless, merchants and manufacturers can create new ways to participate in consumer's in-store moments by designing useful applications and facilitating consumers' research. In the process of doing so, companies can gather information about consumer's interests and concerns, and also gain knowledge of consumers' views of competitors.

Mobile use in retail environments has grown enormously over the past year and is set to explode in 2013. Web shoppers are increasingly using a mobile phone to access retail websites and will even use their phones to compare prices while shopping in person in a store. Product reviews, price comparisons, and recommendations by friends are all playing into the real-time decision making experience.

Information is flowing the other direction as well as consumers broadcast their in-store experiences to their social networks (and the public at large), amplifying good or bad experiences and influencing future visitors.

Companies need to identify the place in the shopping experience that can be complemented with a mobile experience, and how to present a compelling proposition in a world of price transparency. Making your own online experiences mobile ready, building mobile experiences into your store displays, and facilitating research are three places to start.

First, imagine the shopper at a competitor's store or looking at a competing product. Is your website and online commerce experience completely accessible from the most common smartphones so that a comparison can be made? Do you make it easy to understand the advantages your product has over a competitor's?

When you provide information in-store, is it readily accessible from a mobile device? Can a potential buyer go further and see reviews or recommendations by other purchasers? Provide as much information as possible, even when it isn't all positive and make it easy to find your mobile site about a product or you'll find your customers looking at competitors' websites to make their comparisons.

In some cases, an in-store experience may include ordering, payment, providing feedback, participating in loyalty programs, and so on. Determine the right set of services to offer in a mobile experience for your product or service.

Finally, think about how your mobile experience can help connect your customers to others. Social shopping can bring a group of potential customers to your store together. Displaying preference information can lead to gift purchases. Design a mobile-social experience that makes sense for your brand and product or service.

Embrace Transparency

It is not only at the electronics store or the auto dealer that a new consumer power is manifesting itself and changing market dynamics. The e-patient movement is a growing consumer voice for more transparency and more patient control of information in the health-care industry. Efforts by government organizations are making more and better data available about every aspect of the industries they regulate and about their own operations. Nonprofits are publishing extensive data about their fundraising and spending. Companies, too, will find an increased expectation and demand from consumers to be open and transparent about business practices, product contents, pricing, service and support policies, and virtually everything else about their businesses.

In 2012, people have unprecedented access as consumers, as citizens, and as community members to information about companies, products, government, and neighborhoods. This may make organizations uncomfortable, especially when established business practices are at odds with these new customer expectations. But opportunities abound for those able to adapt to this new environment.

These three components of the new state of persistent digital engagement will be hard to ADAPT to for many companies and even some individuals. We have thought of customer service for so long as a cost center that turning it on its head as a place to build markets will challenge both customer service and marketing people's capacity for adaptation. Redesigning our retail environments to support digital interactions will be a process of experimentation and evolution that while ultimately leading to success, will also contain blind alleys and frustrations. And this last adaptation—to an organization's will to be transparent and open will challenge almost everything about how we think about business today. It will be uncomfortable, difficult, and time-consuming to get these things right. But what are your options? If your competitors are doing these things and your customers are demanding them, can you afford to not ADAPT?

CHAPTER

Digitization

The Rising Value of Information in Products and Services

An important shift has slowly gathered momentum over the past 100 years in the way technology proliferates through different aspects of our society. Historically, technology was developed by and for governments (often the military). In the industrial age, technology sometimes moved from government use to corporate use but sometimes technology was developed directly for businesses. Consumer use of technologies would typically happen only after government or business use. But today, technology is often being developed for personal use first and will then move back to industry or government.

An example of this scenario is a company that developed a product for backpackers that performs a simple function—utilizing the global positioning system (GPS) network to track the hiker's location while in the woods in case (in an emergency) the hiker requires rescue. The technology on which this innovation depends, the GPS network, is an example of the old model—commercialization of a military infrastructure for civilian use. But now the innovation of the pocket device is going the other direction—companies that operate in dangerous remote locations have discovered that they can use this continuous location-reporting device in order to keep track of (and rescue if necessary) their employees. A consumer innovation is being embraced by industry.

Innovation Drivers

This is happening because of a simple economic principle of scale and the power of information as a driver for innovation. In the GPS example, a company might purchase hundreds, or at most thousands, of such tracking devices. But a consumer market is measured in millions—with a resulting dramatic reduction in the cost of such a solution. Thus, the company can benefit from consumer-scale efficiencies if the consumer product is good enough for industrial applications. And because the primary innovation driver for this product is information, the product can be developed for that consumer market at very low cost, outside big research and development departments and budgets.

Central to this story is this ascension of bits over atoms—the rising importance of information in the overall value we derive from products. The cost of manufacturing a physical product can decline as more efficient materials, designs, and manufacturing processes are adopted. However, when information becomes a part of the product, the pace of transformation in value radically changes. Information content both changes a product's capabilities and how we use the product. Add to this equation the pace at which semiconductors are shrinking, network throughput is increasing, and wireless communication is becoming cheap and easy. As a result of these changes, products are becoming services, and our appreciation of those products is increasingly dominated by that service component.

Without the mobile phone as a remote control for our world, this transformation wouldn't be happening. Sensors and wireless communications built into our cars and our houses and the products we use would have no value if those things didn't have something to connect to—to transmit their data and provide access to configure and to control. Thus, the capacities for information processing, storage, and communication that are growing in the world, the social mobile cloud, create the value (and demand) for adding a digital layer to every product.

With a smartphone in my hand, I am the master of my universe—to the extent that my universe is also smart. A handheld computer with wireless connectivity generates demand for sensors and wireless connectivity in the products I use, my vehicles, my home, and my office. This leads to a number of important changes in the way we interact with the world and how we in our companies conceive of products and how we deliver them to our customers.

Wireless Sensors in Everything and Everywhere

Imagine a sensor for your running shoe—it keeps track of how far and how fast you have run. But the real magic is in what happens when you upload that data to a website. There you can compare your most recent run with past runs, compare to others, compete or collaborate with friends and strangers, and exchange tips about running. Your shoes become a gateway to a community of runners, and they facilitate the experience of being a part of that community.

Or imagine having control of your home alarm system on your smartphone, including the ability to control lights, appliances, temperature, and door locks and to stream live video from the cameras in your home or business. While products have been available for home automation for years, having a smartphone to control an automated home is finally driving up the demand for these products.

Auto manufacturers are beginning to provide remote access and vehicle information through smartphones. One of the first applications is in electric cars where it is exceptionally useful to know whether your car has finished charging without having to go to wherever it is parked and plugged in.

This digitization trend isn't limited to products. Service providers are also finding ways to embed mobile devices and even wireless sensors into the way they do business. Some quick-service restaurants and coffee shops are providing automation from mobile devices, allowing customers to preorder and prepay for their drinks or food before even arriving at the restaurant location. Adaptive signage that is actuated by pressure (foot traffic) or other kinds of sensors is beginning to appear in retail environments. Entries to entertainment venues are increasingly monitored by cameras that are capable of detecting not only how many people are entering the establishment but also whether those entering are adults or children, and based on the speed of motion, what the wait time might be in a particular line.

Leading companies are reimagining how products become services by integrating information systems into cloud environments where predictive analytics or social connections can add substantial value to the business or customer of those products. They're also reimagining how services can become richer and more valuable using these same technologies. Quick diagnosis of problems, predictive service alerts, and product development insights are just a few of the benefits such companies are realizing.

Application Programming Interfaces for Everything

Exposing all of these data—not just to the company's own applications but also to third parties—is becoming an essential part of deriving value from digitization. Application programming interfaces (APIs) provide a standard way for companies to take data in a shoe or a house or a car and make it available to others who may have creative ideas on how the data can be used.

Perhaps the best-known example of this trend is in our smartphones, which have attracted hundreds of thousands of developers. These companies have effectively harnessed billions of dollars in other people's research and development resources to extend the capabilities of their products—at zero financial risk to themselves. Every company goes through the twin problems of innovation:

1. We have 20 ideas but we can only fund 2 or 3 of them. How do we choose?
2. All of our ideas come from people inside our industry. How do we get out-of-the-box thinking?

An innovation ecosystem powered by APIs can deliver powerful answers to both of these questions. Design incentives and the business model correctly and you can attract people from widely varied backgrounds to invent new customer experiences on your product-as-a-platform all at no financial risk but with your company benefiting from all of the innovation.

Software Is Everywhere

The value of the bits (or software) is rapidly increasing and displacing the value of atoms in our products. This has been happening for some time in industries that are very information intensive such as consumer electronics. But now the trend is impacting shoemakers, car rental agencies, quick-service restaurants, and literally everything else that we buy and use. The ability to embed software into everything, and easily connect to the cloud, will transform every product and service.

As a result, industry after industry is being reinvented through software. And often incumbents are falling to startups that are able to erase traditional barriers to entry into established markets through innovative software—leveraging the social mobile cloud. It is a strategy that incumbents, mired in their industrial era organizational structures and processes, are finding difficult to copy. Experience is making it hard to ADAPT

These three trends—wireless sensors in products, APIs that extend data, and software systems that reorganize the way businesses operate—are a direct challenge to you and your business and a call to action to rethink your value proposition and business model. What will you do if your competitor or a start-up introduces a product tomorrow—just as good but with built-in sensors that add enormous value to the experience of using the product? And connect those customers directly to that competing company in a mutually beneficial ongoing interaction? How long until your unconnected "dumb" product seems uninteresting to buyers who are comparing you with "smart" products that improve the way they work, play, and live, . . . and will it be too late then for you to ADAPT?

8

Crowd Storming, Crowd Sourcing, Collaboration, Co-Creation

People working together to solve problems is not in itself anything new, it is one of the fundamental building blocks of civilization. But the Internet facilitates a kind of crowd collaboration, allowing individuals to more easily come together to discover, to create, to evolve, or simply to complete tasks. Even very complex tasks such as an encyclopedia that was developed entirely through voluntary efforts by individuals, most who don't know one another, and making their contributions from all over the globe.

Simply reducing the friction in communicating and collaborating has made entirely new behaviors possible—crowd-sourced encyclopedia content where an interested amateur might create the initial article but then trained experts (and other amateurs) could join in and help improve the content.

Author Francis Gouillart's book *The Power of Co-Creation* details how companies around the globe are reinventing their businesses by bringing stakeholders together to identify and solve problems in new ways.[1] In a 2011 *Harvard Business Review* article titled "Experience Co-Creation," Gouillart explains that companies must reinvent their existing "inert touch points" into interactive and collaborative experiences. He writes that customer experience must be redesigned:

> By designing engagement platforms—the physical and virtual places through which customers can interact with the company and other stakeholders in order to design their own personalized

experience. The four types of interaction a company typically offers—through its products, its people, the physical places it does business, and the digital sites it possesses—can be made into such engagement platforms.[2]

There are three fundamental changes in thinking that the capacity for interaction and engagement must bring to the way a company thinks about how its own employees interact or how they work with trading partners or ultimately how they engage with customers and prospects:

More People = Faster and Better Decisions

You can make better decisions faster by involving more people. This involvement can be achieved by aggregating information from individuals and learning through the collective views or by allowing people to build on one another's ideas collaboratively. At one company where a prediction network was used to allow employees to collaborate in predicting future quarter sales results, the crowd was consistently better than the economists employed to predict results. Companies are finding enormous benefits in improving analysis, increasing the quality of solutions, and therefore arriving at better decisions by getting more people involved in these processes.

Group Collaboration = Faster and Better Outcomes

When you create an opportunity for people to work together, the work is done more quickly, more easily, and at a higher quality. With the right incentives in place, people will happily contribute and produce unanticipated outcomes. Sometimes called generative systems, the goal is to design interaction systems that encourage positive behaviors and discourage negative behaviors. Attract enough people to participate and the system is up and running and where it goes is only limited by the imagination of the participants and the flexibility of the platform. As the encyclopedia project showed, you might accidentally create the most complete and most valuable compilation of human knowledge ever.

Extend Engagement and You Increase Value for Everyone

Every point of interaction is an opportunity to extend engagement and increase value for all participants. Your company's products, people, places you do business, and digital sites are all capable of providing an engagement platform that enhances a customer's experience and connects customers to your brand, thereby increasing loyalty and advocacy.

Making better and faster decisions, achieving better outcomes, and creating deeper and more meaningful relationships with your customers are within your grasp but will require adaptation of your current thinking and business processes. It is comfortable to be the authority, it feels good to make decisions, and by contrast it does not feel good to discover that a group of nonexperts is capable of making a better decision than you. The idea that a group of random people can come together and produce something of high quality flies in the face of our beliefs about professionalism and expertise. And a commitment to create deep engagement with customers at every opportunity sounds both difficult and expensive. But adapting to these new conditions can come more quickly when you measure the benefits. What is the measurable value to your business to be able to make better decisions faster or to achieve better outcomes? Do you track measures of customer referral value? How do you track customer loyalty? In the chapters ahead, we will explore how different parts of your business will change to help support adaptation to these new conditions.

Notes

1. Venkat Ramaswamy and Francis Gouillart, *The Power of Co-Creation: Build It with Them to Boost Growth, Productivity, and Profits* (New York: Simon & Schuster), 2010.
2. Francis Gouilliart, "Experience Co-Creation," *Harvard Business Review*, HBR Blog Network, April 18, 2011, http://blogs.hbr .org/cs/2011/04/experience_co-creation.html.

CHAPTER

9

Hierarchy Will Yield to Networks, Remaking Organizations

In the world of expensive communications and coordination, we developed hierarchical organizations that neatly separated functions from one another. The bigger the organization, the more silos existed—marketing, sales, research and development, operations, finance—and perhaps separated by region, territory, country . . . every transaction needed processes and controls. Customer service is a process for managing communications with outside parties—people that had actually purchased products from your company. Procurement is a process for managing how you buy from other companies. These organizational structures and processes thrive on two models of value for the individuals that run them—seniority and control of information.

Seniority and Control of Information

Social technology erodes both seniority and control of information. The value that exists in a hierarchical organization from holding information gives way to value from maintaining connections in a networked organization. Information seekers will navigate around information hoarders and find other ways to get the data or knowledge they seek. People helping to make those connections—from one person to another—thrive on this networked information model. A network node through which information and connections flow will be more valuable to an organization than one where information or

75

connections stop or slow. And the individual who is at that node will derive the most from being the person through which the information and connections flow.

Over time as organizations evolve from hierarchical to networked, seniority gives way to connections as a basis for importance. The more connections you have and the more you use those connections to help others, the more important you become. Thus, the most important quality in a successful social enterprise employee is the desire to share information—as opposed to the old hierarchical industrial organization where the incentives are aligned to hoard information.

In the new organization, power (and value) comes from sharing. The more you share, the more you become someone people turn to in the network as a resource. And making yourself a strong network node is the secret to success in the social enterprise, because the stronger your connections are, the more information you will receive as well—ultimately, anyone can be smart. However, the people who are smart *and* who have access to the most information make the best decisions. So share everything and everything will be shared with you. Connect to everyone and everyone will connect to you. Be the brightest light and you will also create the most value for yourself and your organization.

One of the first places that the impact of this transformation to a networked organization will be felt is in the part of the company closest to the customer—marketing, sales, and service. Because the primary impact of the social mobile cloud is to reduce the cost of communication, it makes sense that the first areas of businesses to feel that impact will be the ones where the primary focus is to communicate. Almost every marketing organization is at some stage of the journey from a focus on traditional media and the twentieth-century marketing focus on buying attention to digital media and the new focus on creating relationships and earning engagement.

It would be a mistake to think that the impact will stop at this customer facing activity. While our initial experiences of these new technologies have been as consumers and citizens, increasingly we are bringing these tools into business environments. As digital consumers, we arrive at work with a new set of expectations about what our companies will provide and allow to help us get our jobs done. We expect greater collaboration with our colleagues. We are demanding more transparency both in information and in decisions from management. We believe that we have a greater role to play in solving problems and making decisions. We want technology to use in doing our work that is at least as good as that which we use at home or at school.

This last point is an interesting one as you consider how to ADAPT your business to the new world of the social mobile cloud. The term *consumerization of IT* is more often associated with employees demanding that their companies change. But a simple definition is simply the process by which technology becomes so simple that it can be acquired, configured, and used directly by the end user without the mediation of technical experts. In the social mobile cloud era, the technology that is available for us to acquire and use directly is increasingly powerful—often more powerful than what the companies themselves offer employees.

This consumerization of IT trends will have a profound effect on business over the next decade, challenging the assumptions of information systems and CIO control and giving an increasing amount of power to employees. In the most advanced companies, the role of the CIO is already changing—from a focus on IT operations, cost control, and program management to a role of supporting business requirements, new business models, and revenue growth through the right orchestration of applications and services from external vendors and a technical focus on seamless integration of disparate data sources connected to a growing variety of edge access platforms and applications.

For organizations that do not make this leap, employees will find their own ways to communicate more freely with one another. If companies don't provide the infrastructure to facilitate these conversations, employees will simply adapt commercial services to these needs. This is probably already happening in your organization, perhaps led by younger employees accustomed to using online collaborative applications. They simply continue to use them, not taking seriously the guidance from IT departments that such services constitute a security risk. Carefully defining risk and how it can be managed in the social mobile cloud is another subject for a later chapter.

Finding New Business Model Solutions

One of the implications of all this communication will be to disrupt the traditional barriers between what we think of as inside and outside of organizations. Why shouldn't someone in the finance department comment on marketing plans if she has a great idea? Why can't an external business partner make a suggestion about an internal HR policy if his company has previously dealt with a similar problem and come up with a great solution?

As we mentioned in Chapter 8, we all get smarter faster when we have more inputs from a more diverse group of people. The challenge in the past has been that communication was expensive. Imagine this outlandish scenario—outlandish in a pre-Internet world—how would you ask your external business partners for input into your internal HR policies—and why would they would agree to provide such input? Would you have a conference call and invite them all to join in and listen to the litany of problems your company was trying to address? Would you hold a meeting and invite them to attend a daylong session to review and discuss HR policy best practices? But with the networked, free communication world, the problem can be easily posed to a broad array of people and useful suggestions could come from anywhere. In the networked world, the conversation about HR policy becomes a small side conversation in a broader set of conversations about everything else your businesses are doing and how to do them better.

The next step beyond the network of employees and trading partners will be for organizations to have broader and more open communications with customers and prospective customers. By connecting each of the stakeholder groups, organizations can evolve from closed, sealed enterprises to a new model: the permeable enterprise. Instead of managing communications through rigid process and structure, employees in this new model freely interact with trading partners and customers, participating in engagement platforms designed to bring out the best in participants.

Arriving at this new state will require enormous changes in individual attitudes, business processes, organizational structures, and the technical infrastructure to support all of these changes. Adapting personally and organizationally will start with understanding the new business models we will need to examine in the social mobile cloud. The next few chapters explore examples of these new business models.

CHAPTER 10

How We Buy

Redefining Shopping and Payment

There you are, standing in the sports equipment store swinging the latest club from your favorite manufacturer. You love the club and you're ready to buy. Do you whip out your wallet? Or your phone?

Business Model Shift 1: For Retailers, the Customer Is in Control

Increasingly, consumers are pulling out their phones at the point of sale, finding out whether that big screen TV, pair of designer shoes, or the latest driver at the pro shop can be purchased at a lower price around the block or online and delivered by mail within a few days. In every product category, online sales are increasing and physical retail locations are under pressure.

There is a fundamental shift under way in consumer's expectations of the purchase experience. The old funnel of consumer demand translating to a purchase decision has been permanently disrupted. Access to information, peer opinion, alternative purchase mechanisms, direct connections to manufacturers, and new loyalties to online merchants have tilted the playing field away from even the largest retailers. The customer is in control.

If you are a retailer this raises a host of new challenges in a marketplace where you have already been challenged by the economic downturn, where increased debt to savings ratios has impacted consumption, and the overall low consumer confidence has kept people out of shops. But now on top of all this, a more efficient purchase and delivery mechanism, complete market information, and new more efficient sales and delivery mechanisms have emerged that allow customers to make better choices and obtain the products they want at a lower price than in the established retail stores.

Consumers may still want to come into your store to try on the shoes or swing the golf club. However, when it comes time to make the purchase, how will you make sure that the purchase happens at your store? Convenience and immediacy is no longer enough. With a mobile phone in her pocket, you know she can now find the price of that product at a dozen other stores and online sites and will know that your price, with the cost of real estate and sales associates, is higher than what she can get elsewhere.

So what will become of retailers? Or at least, what will become of their stores? For years now, as I have met with large retailers, I have asked them to rethink their position in the value chain—are you the representative of the manufacturer or the agent of the customer? These two positions are not entirely mutually exclusive but which one you choose as dominant is certain to have a significant impact on everything you do in your business.

Scenario 1: Manufacturer's Representative

In this traditional position, the retailer's job is to promote the manufacturer's products to the customer. As a partner to the manufacturer, revenue is derived from being the most effective representative—the retailer gets greater discounts for higher volume, will be paid for special displays or shelf space, and receives co-marketing dollars. The job of the retailer is to sell as much of the manufacturer's products as possible to the public and to represent the manufacturer's claims to that public. Loyalty to the manufacturers yields rewards for the retailer.

Representation can be exclusive or partial. An example of exclusive representation by a retailer is the dealer networks that auto manufacturers have developed to deliver their products to market. A partial representation example is a grocery store that charges brands for shelf space. In both cases, the retailer is compensated for representing the manufacturer and is aligned with the manufacturer's interests.

Where does the customer fall in this equation? If in this new world the customer is in control, how does she trust you when she knows you represent the manufacturer's interests and not hers?

Scenario 2: Agent for the Customer

A new model is emerging for retailers to focus on being an agent for the customer. Instead of selling the customer what the manufacturer wants to have sold, can a retailer take the side of the customer? Instead of profiting most when the manufacturer's needs are met, can a retailer profit most when the customer's needs are put first? Help the customer select the best product from a range of manufacturers? Help the customer get satisfaction from the manufacturer if there is a problem? In truth, retailers have always been a blend of both—no retailer survives without some focus on the needs of the customer—but making a wholesale switch in approach to placing the customer in the dominant position has until recently been limited to luxury goods and niche markets. Digital expands the potential for this new business model. Here are the three key ingredients to take into consideration when building the customer-centric retailer:

1. Be a trusted source of information
2. Advocate for your customer
3. Design for loyalty

In building your new retail strategy, you may find that the entire design of your current model is wrong—you have too much retail space in the wrong places. You worry too much about what is in stock and not enough about what is available. Your employees are compensated on sales, not on customer satisfaction. But there are new models emerging that are worth learning from.

Companies are creating new retail experiences that are optimized for conversation and learning. You won't see anyone walking through aisles of goods, serving as their own warehouse staff as they find products and drop them into a basket. Instead, the goods are all in back and the retail space is reserved for tables where you can actually put your hands on the products. And as you try out that new laptop, there is a cheerful well-trained employee at the ready to explain the differences between products and the options available. This staff member isn't being compensated to sell you a more expensive product—the questions he or she asks you are about what you want to do with the product, with the end goal to recommend the best product for you.

And when it comes time to purchase, the product is brought to you from the back and the transaction is handled at the same table—no long checkout line. If you have a problem, come back anytime and the staff will patiently help you to correct the problem, replace the product, refund your money, and so on. This is a retail experience that embodies all three ingredients: trusted source of information, customer advocate, and designed for loyalty.

All of this high-touch retail magic is enabled by technology. Companies building these new retail environments have developed a sophisticated set of tools that allow customers and staff to interact efficiently—online appointment reservations, handheld computers that manage waiting lists for walk-in sales assistance, inventory control, and enabling every sales associate to be a walking cash register. And perhaps most important, a detailed customer record and product record that staff can access to help sort out a problem: Is it still under warranty? Have you had problems with it before?

Total digital awareness is essential for the new customer-centric retailer, and the tools to provide this awareness must be in the hands of the sales staff. Make your staff superhuman. They must be more knowledgeable than your customer, they must be empowered to solve your customer's problems, and they must delight your customer with the speed and ease by which those problems are solved.

Even with this level of customer service—and even with the ingredients of information, advocacy, and design for loyalty—we will see an enormous percentage of all purchases shift online. Every retailer should be preparing for this and should be focused on providing an integrated set of online experiences. Customers will increasingly expect a multichannel interaction with companies—in a store, online, on a mobile phone, in a social network whenever the customer wants the interaction.

Business Model Shift 2: Pay from the Comfort of Your Own Phone

If you aren't pulling out your phone to shop online, you may be pulling it out to pay. Companies are in a race to own the new digital wallet. Collectively their efforts are conditioning consumers to use smartphones to pay for everything with the ultimate vision: the elimination of the plastic card. Eventually, you should be able to tap an app on your smartphone and pay for things in all sorts of retail environments.

There are a multitude of players with pieces of the all-digital, mobile MONEY 2.0 puzzle: payment systems vendors, merchant loyalty program developers, virtual mall builders. It will take a few years for money as we know it to change forever. And there are issues to hammer out, not the least of which is whether these new systems have adequate security for transferring money value in the ether, when and how the necessary additional hardware will show up on merchant counters, and how quickly we will feel comfortable pulling out our phones instead of our wallets to pay. But MONEY 2.0 is inevitable and on its way. Businesses need to spend the next few years in development for MONEY 2.0, with interim offerings along the way. This is an enormous opportunity for all business leaders, even beyond retailers.

The most essential thing to understand about MONEY 2.0: There is absolutely no reason that our future should contain plastic cards, paper, or coins as money. And one step further—our very idea of what money is will explode. The reason an all-digital stored value mobile payment app can work, and will be one of the most compelling reasons for those without smartphones to buy them over the next few years, is that the relationship between consumers and merchants is about to be transformed by corporate sponsored currency.

Corporate-Sponsored Currency: In Business We Trust

Corporate-sponsored currency and its applications will not only change the way you think about conducting your business but will also change what it means to conduct business altogether.

Regardless of whether we use a card or an app to pay for something, we still think of money as being backed by a sovereign state. But if we examine stored value (money) and pricing (the exchange of stored value for goods), we find that these concepts are permeable in an entirely digital world. And so the definition of money is changing, or should I say changing back?

You could look at money (remember, stored value) backed by corporations as an evolution, but in a certain sense we are going full circle, back to the days of bartering hay for sheep. The only difference now is the delivery system. By the way, herein lie a critical conceptual element of the social mobile cloud and reinventing your business. It is not the product or idea that is outdated, rather it is the delivery system and all the new inherent possibilities given by that delivery system that change.

Even after sovereign currency had come to dominate financial transactions, there continued to be corporate sponsored currency, from blue chip stamps to barter between farmers. To understand the current iteration of corporate-sponsored currency is to understand how the manifestations of digital money are evolving. Think about what might happen if you could use a coffee shop stored value card elsewhere—when you earn that free tenth cup of coffee, you could trade the value of that coffee for other products. Stored value is stored value. Digital transactions make this value exchange even more fluid than money did.

To understand this concept, it is worthwhile to take a moment to reflect more on the evolution of this medium we take for granted today, money.

It is rather inconvenient to haul hay around everywhere you go, or to lead your sheep to each merchant from whom you wish to buy something. And not everyone you want to do business with wants hay or sheep. But if your livelihood depends on growing hay or raising sheep, that is the value you have to offer for the other goods you need. Commerce demands a more convenient medium by which the value of hay and the value of sheep can be represented and thus exchanged. This is Economics 101, but sometimes it is worthwhile to reflect on how we arrived at the current state of things.

The first stage in the process of developing markets was to utilize precious materials that could be more easily transported than the goods they represented. The exchange of gold or silver facilitated financial transactions but was ultimately limited by the weight and value of the underlying metal. Paper and nonprecious coin currencies were issued to represent gold and silver stored in bank vaults and ultimately in government vaults as the power to issue was consolidated by sovereign governments.

And then a remarkable thing happened in the twentieth century—the value of a government-issued currency was disassociated from underlying physical assets (gold or silver), and our notion of currency evolved to depend on instruments that were backed solely by trust in a sovereign government.

Today, we ask every producer of goods and services and every consumer of those goods and services to suspend disbelief about the value of the instrument we use to value those goods and continue to accumulate, exchange, and trust in that instrument—even though it has no ultimate connection to an underlying specific physical asset that we can rely on as providing a determinant of its value. It is now entirely about the belief that the issuer of the currency will have the ability to defend the value of that currency over time—through the strength of its political system, economic system, and military.

Whether you individually object to or approve of this new floating currency backed only by trust in sovereign governments, as a collective the world now conducts its business on the basis of trust alone. Which has in turn established a new dynamic—a willingness to trust in entities other than governments.

Business Model Shift 3: Corporate Currencies

Once we place our trust in one kind of entity (a government), what stops us from placing our trust in another kind of entity (a corporation)? The mechanism for ascribing value is almost the same, and our willingness to place our trust in an entity rationally should be associated simply with our trust in the entity that has made the promise. Will they live up to the obligation to which they have committed?

Airline loyalty programs are one kind of corporate-sponsored currency with which we are already quite comfortable. These programs have expanded well beyond an accumulation of points toward a free flight and now points can be used to buy any kind of product. Travelers can use their accumulated frequent flier miles to buy goods and services even while in transit. Think of an airline that is the equivalent of a mall full of goods and services, with a captive audience, distribution channel, and, if need be, a transportation system.

Financial institutions are issuing points in exchange for using their payment mechanism, encouraging our dependence on their particular card by rewarding us in an alternative corporate-backed currency that can then be used to purchase goods or services. Are these discounts? Loyalty programs? Currencies? These are all shades of the same underlying function as they all speak to the exchange of value between two parties in which a seller provides value to a buyer.

There will be an increasing number of corporate-sponsored currencies, games, points, reward systems, and they will be completely digital and mobile from the outset. I have emphasized and reemphasized building infrastructure for mobile because it is the driving force of doing business in this new marketplace—in large part because of the ability to redefine the medium of exchange. Having dozens or hundreds of currencies with a physical manifestation (even a plastic card) is unwieldy. But digitally stored, completely mobile corporate sponsored currency, which by definition has value limited only by a corporation's willingness to set up games and reward players, will change the economics of our transactions and decisions on whom we transact with—and we can entertain a menagerie of such currencies when they are all managed on (and by) our smartphones.

Lest you limit your thinking to customer interactions, let me briefly mention that such currencies can be used across every part of your business. Leveraging your existing customer base, business partners, and employees can all be a part of a corporate currency program. In a supply chain, simple inventory management enabled by the social mobile cloud can easily become a stock exchange for goods and services, including settlement of transactions, which could potentially lead to a sophisticated bartering program. Employees can engage in micro-transactions with one another connected to performance recognition and new systems are developing that allow organizations to more easily track goals, teamwork, individual contributions, and so on.

Of course, such exchanges will not be immune to taxation and governments will have to evolve regulations in order to capture their share of all of this activity. But since the transactions will be entirely digital, tracking them will be the easy part.

The evolution of MONEY 2.0 in terms of merchandising programs, loyalty programs, and virtual corporate currencies will evolve in step with the *gamification* of selling and buying goods and services in the social mobile cloud. Chapter 11 will address the specifics of what gamification means and the implications for businesses. For the moment, focus on how a corporate-sponsored currency changes how you engage with your customers.

Corporate versus Sovereign Currency?

The moment I mention buying something like a real life car with virtual currency a new set of questions arise. The car has real value and to buy one often means putting up some part of the value in cash and then leasing or taking an interest-bearing loan for the balance. This process is conducted in a sovereign-backed currency because all of the participants in the transaction understand how that currency functions in the larger economy. Manufacturer, dealer, financial institution, insurance company—all stakeholders in an auto purchase—agree that one U.S. government-issued dollar is worth some specific amount at a particular moment in time and that the value is relatively stable forward and backward in time.

It is important to understand that corporate-issued virtual currencies do not offer an alternative to the existence of sovereign-backed currencies. Without getting philosophical about the evolution of civil societies, I will simply assert that as long as we live in physical spaces we'll need governments, and that governments will have the power to determine how and when we exchange value in those physical spaces. Governments derive their authority in part from money and therefore need to keep control of money. It is even written into the U.S. Constitution and the laws of virtually every country that the government has the sole authority to issue fungible currency.

There are many complex systems of value creation and destruction that give (or take away) power from sovereign states. And there are so many practices entwined with every aspect of our lives—lending and the interest paid by borrowers, complex insurance mechanisms—that sovereign currency will remain an essential part of how our society functions.

However, it is equally difficult for sovereign governments to withhold the ability to issue corporate currencies and this gets to the heart of what is different about a virtual currency from what we have historically thought of as money. The problem is entwined in the very concept of currency as a symbolic representation of value. Offering a coupon is in a sense issuing a currency (albeit of limited use). Loyalty programs are currencies in disguise. Companies who adjust their price for their best customers or reward frequency of purchase are all to some degree issuing a currency.

Some corporations are even starting to innovate around the complexity of multiple sovereign currencies, particularly for the wealthiest class of consumers. Some banks already have a hybrid currency if you are really wealthy: The bank allows their top clients to store value (their money) at a world balanced currency price. Think of it as a better dollar, insulated from local business cycles and political events—it is made up of a representation of all the world's currencies balanced by the size and stability of their economies.

Business Model Shift 4: Insuring Corporate Currencies

One new subindustry we may see is the rise of new insurance products for corporate-sponsored currencies, for corporations such as airlines to provide assurance for the points held in their systems. If consumers are going to store value in miles or other corporate currencies, they may want more reassurance that their "money" is safe. Not that everyone will bother to take out this new insurance—one airline executive prodded me with this query: "Would you feel more comfortable with your money in a sovereign currency or in our airline currency?"

Nevertheless, insurance will provide a broader market for virtual currencies. The local dealership is a lot more likely to sell you a car in exchange for points when it has some recourse for the exchange of those points if the issuer defaults. Insurance and banking have always been close cousins and the realm of virtual currencies will only continue to build connective tissue as issues of value, stability, security, and exchange all arise with the growth in corporate currencies.

A smartphone is now every person's conduit between his or her money and any merchant; the phone conducts the transaction. Money as we have always known it—paper, coins, plastic, and more paper in the form of checks—is simply a physical representation of stored value. Now we can access that stored value digitally because consumer, merchant, and bank can transact seamlessly. Stored value between different units—dollars, euros, miles, points—can all be calculated within the smartphone and determining the optimal place to make a purchase and mix of currencies to make up that purchase will be one of the important functions our phones provide.

Business Model Shift 5: Accepting (Multicurrency) Mobile Payments

Armed with our smartphones and an Internet connection, we will no longer have a need to carry cash once all merchants, professional services companies, and government agencies are set up to accept mobile payments.

There is a lot of impetus for businesses to accept mobile payments. It requires a lot less of a hardware investment, and social networking via smartphones means attracting customers that businesses would never otherwise find. For small businesses and new businesses, you can say good-bye to cash registers and point of sale (POS) terminals. A laptop or even a tablet is the new cash register. Large businesses have hefty investments in this POS hardware, so retooling for mobile might be a shorter term solution, but ultimately all brick-and-mortar retailers will have every employee carrying a smartphone, and no cash register in sight.

There are clear, systematic strategies for this migration path that large businesses and small businesses alike need to know, the critical aspect of which is building any payment system for long-term mobile use. You want all of your customers, including employees, business-to-business partners, and retail consumers, to be able to use their smartphone remote control to pay you, get paid by you, receive bonuses, loyalty programs, discounts, and exclusive offers.

Everyone Will Be a Superhero When Apps Are the New Plastic

Mobile money will also change the way you use money. Think of every place you shop as an app on your phone. Then there is an app that will be the new debit, credit, or even ATM card. So you have your general money account and lines of credit as one icon and merchant icons representing a certain amount of stored value. Remember, value won't be defined as just straight cash. Your coffee shop value might include a tenth free cup of coffee, exclusive offers, or discounts on special orders (like soy milk).

With a smartphone, opportunities become limitless for merchant loyalty programs, exclusive discounts, and even transferrable savings. If your spouse is browsing at the brick-and-mortar bookstore one day, you can send his or her smartphone a discount offer that you had stored on an app on your phone. You send it while your spouse is shopping, and he or she can then use the discount on the spot. That will work in the physical world or the online world.

Ultimately, our wealth will be a combination of our sovereign currency savings, assets, collected virtual currencies, and access to credit which, will all be managed by a set of smart agents in the cloud and accessible from our mobile devices when and where we need precisely the right mix of these different stored values. Money provided a simplification to ease transactions. However, the social mobile cloud allows complexity to grow while presenting itself in a simple guise.

Business Model Shift 6: Transforming the Purchase Experience with Mobile Payments

Imagine how changing the purchase mechanism will change our experience of the purchase process: airport lines, rental car lines, grocery stores, any transaction line whatsoever. Right now you can purchase an airplane ticket and download a mobile boarding pass from the comfort of your own home (or the comfort of your own phone) and then use the scanners at airport security and the gate to board the plane. The next step is to add this intelligence to the rest of the process. Why not also have self-checking luggage? Some airlines are already attaching smart tags to bags that identify the owner and track the bag's location in real time. Mobile payment lets you scan your own bag, drop it on a conveyer belt, and away it goes—tracked by you, paid for by you, and with the same likelihood of reaching your destination at the same time as you (with hope that this will improve as well!)

And what is the purpose of the line at a rental car place? Already eliminated for frequent renters, the casual traveler should be able to process everything by mobile as well. On the shuttle bus to get the car, you should be able to check in on your smartphone, pay, and go straight to the lot, with an assigned lot number, to pick up the car. On the way out, scan the appropriate mobile bar code, which confirms that everything has been accomplished correctly, including an identifying code transmitted by the car. Then the mechanical arm on the checkout booth lifts, and you're on your way.

Everything we do as citizens, customers, and employees will be changed by the ubiquity of computing and network connectivity to payment mechanisms. What about doctors' offices and the entire mind-numbing insurance loop of payment? Is there any reason you cannot personally transact this bureaucracy from an app? No. Those forms you send in, finding the co-pay, all of that tedious paperwork is obsolete. And when it comes to processes like health insurance coverage and reimbursements, the length of time it will take doctors and patients alike to get paid will be significantly shorter.

In some industries, there is a perception that the "float" between request for payment and fulfilling the transaction offers some advantage to the entity that controls the stored value. But the elimination of people and paperwork offers a more compelling advantage to those who streamline these processes. And competitive pressure will drag even the most recalcitrant businesses into wholesale digital transformation. I mention this because if your business is in a similar boat, where slowing down the flow of money is a key revenue stream, you will need to adapt to the fact that the float will be ending soon. There is no point fighting it. You must strategize by factoring the inevitability into your business development plan.

The next time you take a walk in your local retail district, or are out running errands of any kind, ask yourself this: Should I have to wait in a line in order to pay for something? Why do I need money (in the form of cash or credit cards) for anything I have to do? Could I survive with just my smartphone? Why shouldn't I be able to pay for everything with just my smartphone?

With this in mind, start thinking what you could offer your own customers. And when you're envisioning, remember that the implications go far beyond selling products and services to consumers. Also start to think about interaction with government agencies, from renewing a driver's license, or city dog license, to paying taxes.

For business to business, your entire supply chain can settle transactions, as well as conduct inventory and supplier management this way. Employee relationships? The ultimate monetary tie for any business can now be seamless, and provide employees with perks that don't even add to your expenses. Shouldn't your business be an app on a smartphone that all of your business partners, regulators, employees, and customers can access for communication, collaboration, and commerce?

CHAPTER

11

The Game of Work, the Work of Game

In Chapter 10, I talked about virtual currency and how they could be used to change the way customers think about transactions and how you use them in loyalty programs. But now think in terms of that next bonus to employees: What if they could earn virtual currency in your corporate environment? Could they buy vacations, electronics, and new cars with co-marketing and barter agreements your company sets up? Could you reward them for collaboration, good ideas, or staying healthy?

Business Model Shift 7: Turning Work into a Game

In terms of perks and bonuses for employees—which could also apply to rewarding good suppliers and other business partners: What if you could give them virtual money that has value to them but allows you to encourage them to buy certain things or behave in certain ways?

Imagine this virtual currency integrated into an employee mobile app—a remote control for work. What if any employee could click on an app to call in sick to work, make a contribution to a 401k, or apply for an internal position that has opened up? Employees on the road can pay for travel expenses directly from a per diem that settles instantly and dually serves as an expense report. If there is an infraction on an expense report—an unallowable expense—there could be an instant alert, even prohibiting payment, or maybe allowing the more expensive hotel if the employee uses a corporate currency to cover the additional expense. It is the conceptual corporate charge card powered by virtual currency; with a built-in capacity to track expenses, it encourages the right behaviors as a built-in part of the process.

If any chapter in this book defines the scope of the social mobile cloud, it is this one. If any chapter tells business leaders what they ultimately need to do in order to thrive in a social mobile cloud environment, it is this one.

I've talked about games, but let's delve a bit more deeply, because you need to start thinking about creating your own, designed with incentive for stakeholders of all kinds to meet your goals. You need to start thinking like this: What if I could give my kids allowance money that they can only spend at certain merchants in town? What if I could have a healthcare scoring system for my employees—they get points for joining a gym, eating right, stopping smoking. When they accumulate a certain amount of points, they get an extra vacation day. And what if all of this happens in a way that allows them to enjoy the experience?

Games are at the heart of competition, of thriving versus becoming obsolete, of giving people a stake versus shutting them out. Games are the mechanism for business and consumerism. The new iteration of consumer games is a direct result of the reinvention of money and provides a first safe place for experimentation and adoption. Games provide the ability to have digitized stored value and corporate-backed currency and a motivation for people to collect and use that currency. This new marketplace condition that is sometimes called MONEY 2.0 provides an unprecedented opportunity to make goals and standards of behavior an explicit part of *doing*.

It is important to keep this concept in mind as I explain gamification in detail. Traditionally, we communicate goals or standards of behavior ahead of an employee engaging in activities—perhaps as a part of onboarding an employee or through training classes. And we have processes, after the fact, that help us reward or punish employees based on how well they achieved the goals or followed the standards. What happens when we gamify our environments so that the game can reinforce the desired behavior while the employee is working, and the currency can reward (or punish) as the work is done.

Stored value as you remember is a shorthand for money, but money as an app on your smartphone remote control. Stored value can itself be the value proposition once people understand that at some point they can exchange it for something they want. Once that concept becomes clear, people want as much stored value as they can get. And stored value of this kind can be better than cash because it can give us access to things that cash can't buy. It can provide exclusive access, the ability to obtain limited edition items, or nonmonetary benefits.

Digitized stored value doesn't take up space, or mental bandwidth. It makes you feel wealthy since you can see it any time you want right on your screen, and it is a new resource. Who doesn't want as many resources as possible at our fingertips?

So what does that have to do with gamification? Sounds more like elaborate couponing. Well, the conditions of elaborate couponing give rise to gamification because with all that stored value, the stage is set to get people to play to win, to get as much bang for their stored value buck as possible, and to give the incentive to want and need things sooner rather than later.

Put on your consumer hat for a moment: The moment you need to buy something, you want to know how much it is. The moment someone tells you that you need for pay for something, you want to know how much it is. You want to know how to pay the least amount possible but still get the best value.

Instinctively, we can all see that the game is afoot. We live in a world where we cannot buy a cup of coffee without expecting to be rewarded for the act. As a business leader, know that every one of your employees and customers expects your business to provide tangible and intangible rewards. And if you provide good rewards for your stakeholders, you will create loyalty to your company and your products. Games have the ability to give people stake in a situation, and when people have stake, they are invested and attached. That is a winning combination for any business.

Bear in mind an interesting part of this gamification phenomenon. Businesses with smartphone apps tend to have more engaged customers than businesses that rely only on websites. It is part of the remote control mentality: When you have a remote control in your hands, and you click on something, you know that there is intent to trigger action.

Websites, on the other hand, can be just for browsing.

What Is a Game?

Let's step back for a moment and really think about what a game is. A game is a set of rules that everyone knows and under which everyone is treated equally. A game means there are outcomes for following those rules. There is always a system. All games have players and a goal people want; there is a stake in the game, a conflict, and the inherent possibility of either winning or losing. Chess is called the game of life for a reason. With each move, the game changes and there is no certainty, no best move. And the most important aspect for our purposes is that games have a reward if you win.

The caveat: Games aren't always fun. The phrase "you have to play the game" insinuates that life serves up a lot of unpleasant games, such as office politics, jockeying with an insurance company for a payout, adhering to rules you didn't make and which you wouldn't choose. People play far too many games they don't want to play, so it behooves businesses to choose games people will enjoy. I bring this up not because it would be any executive's intent to create a negative game, but many executives inadvertently create negative environments both for their employees and for their customers. It takes a lot of attention to detail and experimentation to design games that are fun.

In the era of the social mobile cloud, you need to think of your employees as valuable customers as well, and so office politics is something that needs to be on your radar. You can even counteract the negativity in corporate cultures with gamification by remembering something incredibly simple: In an abundant society, we use fun as a motivator. Fun is one of the rewards. There is every reason the workplace should be fun and no reason it shouldn't be. If you are playing with your remote control smartphone by now, exploring social networks and new apps, you are already seeing how fun has begun to permeate the relationships we have with other people, even when the context for the relationship is work.

And make no mistake, as a business leader you must create games for all of your stakeholders, both internal and external. The era of gamification is here, and it is time to ADAPT. The good news is that when you embrace gamification, you will learn that games enhance productivity, so it really makes sense from any business perspective.

Examine your own life, and think about things that get done versus those that don't—I think you'll find that incentives play a large role. That truism is why gamification exists to begin with. Do you go to work without being paid? Or do pro bono work without some sense of recognition of a good that you have created? These are ways we all keep score in the game we play every day when we wake up.

The history of games is a long one, as long as history itself. The ancient Greeks and Romans are archetypes for our modern world. Although brutal, their games created a sense of achievement, reward, and rank. They created rules so everyone understood how outcomes were determined and conflict was resolved. The Coliseum was an arena to focus and alleviate aggression. Now we've come a long way. We can add fun to the mix, not merely resolve conflict. Think about any corporation that sponsors employee sports teams. It is the same concept. The physical outlet gives employees release from tension, provides conflict resolution with peers, and is also fun. Keep this in mind as you look at examples of electronic games and the application of gamification in your business.

Games Are Social, So Look at Social Gaming First

Hundreds of millions of people are spending time online playing games in social networks. They manage virtual farms by plowing virtual land, planting, growing and harvesting virtual crops, harvesting the virtual trees and bushes, and raising virtual livestock. People want to play games and they want to play with one another. The content of the game may be trivial, but the social interactions are not. These games (and the companies behind them) are successful because they have learned how to design games that use those social interactions to create greater engagement.

Business Model Shift 8: Data-Driven Decision Making and a Culture of Experimentation

Understand games as both the engagement platform for your customers and the window into their behaviors and desires. What social gaming companies have unlocked is the mechanism for understanding how we are motivated and what a company can do with that knowledge. Successful social gaming companies analyze every aspect of the player's interactions with their games. And the data are provided back to employees to enable decision making.

Imagine being an employee at one of these companies. How would you present this idea in the next management meeting, where you hope to obtain funding and permission to pursue your idea? Would you talk about how other companies had succeeded in building games like the one you describe? Would you talk about your experience in having built similar games? Neither approach will win approval unless it has one additional component—data.

Where are the data to back up your claim that this new idea has merit? What experiments have you run to show that this could work, not in the abstract, but concretely? Where is your plan for incrementally developing your idea based on iterative loops of experimentation, data gathering, analysis, and adjustment to your plans?

Your business will need to start looking a lot more like these businesses with data gathering built into the design of your products and services, iterative decision-making loops that allow you to analyze that data and use it to improve and make faster, better decisions that increase the delight of your customers. Gamification is a way to both create the interactions with your customers that will cause them to give you the data you need and the mechanism by which you will collect this data.

A Mobile Example

There is a class of games on smartphones that you play alone, not against or with other competitors, yet they are a social phenomenon. These games have simple principles—simulated kinetics such as slingshots or swinging ropes—that create a sense of fun and engagement that has people playing for hours, watching each other play, sharing the challenges and fun of solving visual interactive puzzles.

There are six aspects that are important, and fascinating, about these games:

1. They are typically very simple.
2. Anyone can play yet there is a range of game play from easy to very challenging.
3. Both children and adults can enjoy them.
4. The way the games are played invites people to watch each other play (including parents and their children).
5. People are more than happy to pay for them.
6. The reward is solely in the satisfaction of beating the game.

The companies that have developed these games, as with the social games, have studied every aspect of how people interact and used the data they have gathered in order to design more and more engaging products. With each of the successes, there have been many prior attempts that have not succeeded. Understanding how to do iterative product development, experimental design, and the collection and analysis of data are the skills that have helped these companies succeed.

The point of all of these examples is not to suggest that you go into the gaming business. Rather, it is how companies are using data to make better decisions and how game dynamics can be used to create engagement and satisfaction. Each of these is an example of a business that has succeeded by building a data enabled application—embedding into its products the capability to gather information about how the product is being used—in this case, how the game is being played. Ask yourself how your company can collect data about how people use your products or services and how you can develop the discipline to use this data to drive decisions and how to make iterative improvement. Take these concepts to your conference table and ask what experiments you should be running right now.

Getting Started with Employees

Begin this journey with your own employees. In creating a gamification philosophy in your business, focus on two key aspects of creating your own games to get started:

1. Remember that you need to focus on incentive design.
2. Iterate internally first by experimenting on employees, second on partners, and lastly with your customers.

Incentive design means designing the game with built-in encouragements (rewards or penalties) that direct participants toward the outcomes you desire. Gamification is all about incentive design. Some people don't like games, but don't dwell on designing any to try to lure them. The vast majority of people are happy to tally their points and get a reward.

So, how do you go about designing for incentive? Here is a simple acronym to remember—PHAME. Yes, "fame," but don't forget to spell it with a PH. It stands for:

- **Problem**: What is the problem you are setting out to solve?
- **Hypothesis**: What is your idea about how that problem might be solved?

- **Action**: What are the actions you can take to test your hypothesis?
- **Metrics**: How will you measure the outcomes and what goals will you set?
- **Experiment**: Run an experiment and evaluate the results.

A clear problem definition is often the hardest part of this process. You have to define a problem narrowly enough that you can develop a useful hypothesis and action to actually test for a solution. A problem like "we need to generate more sales" will never give you a good start to the PHAME process. Instead, you want something more concrete. "Increase the number of customers that purchase a pastry and coffee instead of just coffee," might be a good starting point. Another example might be, "Encourage additional repeat purchases by existing loyal customers." These problem statements have the benefit of looking at specific products to focus on, or specific customers and desired actions. The more specific you have made the problem statement, the easier it will be to come up with a hypothesis. Even better if the problem includes a defined goal—double repeat sales, for example, is more specific and useful than just seeking additional repeat sales.

This next step, developing a hypothesis, is when you become a scientist. Science is about envisioning a possible answer to a question, but envisioning that answer in a way that is testable. This is where management by instinct and management by data part ways. The discipline to hypothesize is perhaps the most important skill you will use to succeed in the ADAPT process. A hypothesis should be testable in a straightforward way—at the lowest possible cost and in the shortest period of time. In driving more pastry sales to coffee buyers, a hypothesis might be that by having a special box on the coffee shop loyalty card for "coffee plus pastry" customers would think about making that dual purchase.

The PH part of the process is where all the important thinking work gets done. Initially, you will start with a best guess, but this is an iterative process, and over time your PH will improve with data and analytics. But as you move on to AME remember that this will become an iterative process of improvement only if you build data collection into your processes. The action to test our coffee shop idea is simple: All you have to do is print some special loyalty cards that have this additional graphic of a coffee plus pastry purchase. But in order to make sense of the results, you'll need to be counting purchases before you start the experiment so that you'll have something to which you can compare. Metrics is both what you hope the outcome to be (success would perhaps be an additional 10 pastries sold per day) and how you track that outcome. Once all of this has been defined, you can go to the last stage of running the experiment.

And after all that, what happens? You aren't done! Based on your results, you will then iterate on the problem, the hypothesis, the actions, and even the metrics and run the experiment again! This test and iterate approach, the scientific method, is something that people have been using for centuries to develop our understanding of the cosmos, cure diseases, and expand countless other areas of human knowledge. The social mobile cloud now lets us use the scientific method to run our businesses.

Even if your business is not inherently digital like those game companies, you can now use the social mobile cloud to create experiences that will allow you to benefit from this information gathering and analysis loop. And remember, you are retooling your business for mobile, not just that desk-bound Web.

There are at least three reasons to start with your own employees:

1. For the social mobile cloud, remember that you need to clean house and turn all employees into responsible spokespeople for your business. They are spokespeople no matter what because of social networks, so gamification can be a method to make sure what is being said and heard by all is positive. Games that reward employees for positive public outreach ideas and messaging can have quite a return on investment for you: It can accomplish public relations, marketing, and advertising goals—even have direct measurable impact on sales. Go to a business social networking page and look for stellar employee spokespeople. Really study how they engage with others, what they offer the community, which questions they ask, and how others respond.

2. Employees are safer to experiment with than external customers. Also, if a game fails and employees vote on the game's value, it is empowering to them. Employees will feel like they have a voice in the company's decision making. Having a stake creates loyalty.

3. You know where the weak spots in your organization are and can target games to build morale, expertise, and whatever else

those weak spots need. Again, remember in incentive design you keep in mind what your outcome should be and design to it. So, say you need a sales team that is proactive, rather than your present one, which may tend to passively wait for qualified leads, you can create a game that really rewards proactive behavior, cold calling success, or sales strategies. Create a game for finding new leads.

Once you have succeeded in creating games for your employees, games that engage your trading partners come next. Supply chain games are a short leap from employee-focused games—they employ similar thinking and strategies to create and execute them. You want suppliers that are motivated, productive, and loyal. They are external employees in a sense—both they and your direct employees are business partners—the words on their checks may be different and the percentage of the time they focus on you will vary, but ultimately you want both to be working toward the success of your business.

The third phase is the marketplace. You will have your house in order by the time you reach this phase, and you will have experimented with enough games to have insight into the marketplace. The combination of having your employees engaged online and engaging your vendors gives you the key to succeeding with customers—real interactions with real human beings. Customers know how to differentiate between a canned marketing spiel and a passionate employee speaking from his or her heart.

Recently, a large consumer products company that had, over time, developed some negative brand associations asked me what they could do to use social media to improve their reputation. My number one recommendation was to get your passionate employees talking to the marketplace! The company has a great story, good people, wonderful aspirations, and no reason to be distrusted. But the company breeds distrust by trying to control their communications in their marketplace. Don't hide your employees! Get them engaged with the market. A game is a great environment in which to learn how to do this.

Use games to break down this barrier and give your employees and your customers something fun to do together—design the games around achieving objectives that are good for your company and good for your customers. Using stored value, providing fun activities, and creating links between people are all a part of what organizations will have to do to be relevant in the new era of the social mobile cloud.

Learning how to design with fun and incentives in mind is the first step in thinking about the larger domain of engagement platforms. Anything you hope to have happen through the interactions of your stakeholders—whether they are employees, trading partners, or customers—will come as a result of the right engagement platform design. The social mobile cloud has changed expectations: your customers and employees expect to be participants—not subjects—in their interactions with your company. It is no longer acceptable to provide an experience that optimizes only for the company's objectives. Every experience you provide for interaction should inherently delight.

Business Model Shift 9: Experience Is the Dominant Value

You may still believe that your company provides a product. But increasingly the product is merely a component in the total experience. The real work of our companies going forward is to create this total experience. Recall from an earlier chapter the new state of existence—persistent digital engagement. As companies, we can learn to be present in that digital world at the right times to participate in the experiences that our customers have that are relevant to the products and services we offer.

Companies are learning how to do this with every kind of product. For example, there is a life cycle of engagement with running that includes buying shoes as a small component. But the rest of the experience of running is where the really rich experience occurs—and not just the running itself. Deciding where to run, challenging friends, participating in races, comparing results, tracking improvement, and so on. An engagement platform for runners allows the shoemaker to participate in the broader spectrum of the running experiences.

And when a shoemaker sells a runner the sensor to track statistics about a run and provides the online service to store that data and connect to other runners to compare (the social mobile cloud), they are increasingly selling an experience to their customers, not a pair of shoes. There is an important lesson to take away from the emergence of experience as dominant over product in customer interactions.

The best way to understand this is through understanding our hierarchy of needs.

Satisfying our basic needs such as food and shelter naturally takes precedence to more sophisticated needs. But as each requirement is satisfied, we can begin to think about a higher level of needs (companionship, for example). Ultimately, the most important need to satisfy is our own sense of self, self-actualization or the realization or fulfillment of one's own talents and potentialities. This is the stage in which we are able to appreciate meaning. And experience is the crucible in which meaning is formed.

Companies can facilitate the creation of meaning when they are agents in the process of defining experience. In the previous example, it is not just about being present during the run—it's about how a company can facilitate an extension of the running experience by hosting the data online and allowing the runner to evaluate each run in the context of past runs and by comparison to other runners. The experience of running becomes measurable and social. As a result, the runner is able to reflect on the run in entirely new ways and can use the experience of running to connect and collaborate with others, bringing additional meaning and benefits.

Companies will increasingly need to focus on experience and the creation of meaning to create engagement with customers, trading partners, and employees. Can your company compete based just on price or speed? Can you keep up a pace of innovation that allows you to consistently differentiate just on product features? Are your employees satisfied with a paycheck and the knowledge that they created wealth for the company's shareholders or will people increasingly ask "why" and "what else?" Can your company create experiences that add meaning to people's lives? The reinvention of money and gamification provide companies with a new platform for creating value in their interactions with employees, trading partners, and customers.

CHAPTER 12

Work and the Workplace Reimagined

While Chapter 11's description of the importance of gamification was a critical chapter in showing how the social mobile cloud transforms interactions between us (inside and outside of our businesses), this chapter on how the workplace has forever changed is the defining chapter for you personally and your role in the social mobile cloud. We are at the beginning stages of entirely rethinking the way people will work, a profound and historic shift in the employer-employee relationship. You must take a lead in thinking this through for your business, processing how this will change you and your employees and adapting like a visionary. You are either 10 steps ahead or you are obsolete.

Nothing short of a revolution is required—we are all operating in a moment in which the organization is turning inside out and fundamentally new models of organizing work are emerging.

Forces of Change

Two forces of change are simultaneously creating this new work environment.

1. First, as opposed to the history of the Industrial Age in which value was created through the standardization of roles in structured hierarchies, today value is being created through dynamic, self-organizing, and specialized roles—with the contributions of individuals to the production process becoming more differentiated.

An important part of understanding this transition is in understanding the growing role of information as a part of the value of products and services. When the primary value of a product was in its physical form (metal, plastic, cloth, etc.), value was created through the efficient organization of labor to manufacture or assemble those products. But now, the cost of manufacturing products has plummeted at the same time that quality has skyrocketed—so differentiation between competing products is increasingly through design, software, or other information and knowledge-based contributions to the product. This trend has impacted services as well, with an increasing software and data component to making services competitive.

2. Second, technology is allowing work to be done from different places and times and by a broader range of people than we've ever been able to include before—organizing themselves dynamically through networks. This creates the opportunity for employers and employees to form more ad hoc relationships, focused around projects with discrete time horizons and objectives. As mentioned earlier, technology has reduced the cost of communication and the cost of coordination virtually to zero, enabling entirely new organizational structures to emerge, wiping out the clunky hierarchy of the industrial era.

As a result of these two trends, companies and employees have started to think about their roles in new ways. A company might partner with a smaller entity with narrow specialization to fulfill certain kinds of needs rather than directly employing people with that specialization. Or a company might use more temporary staff with specialized skills. While these practices might cost more than employing people directly, the best people might prefer to be independent of large companies—enjoying more flexibility and variety in their work.

Even internally, we must cultivate coach-coachee relationships rather than relationships determined by level. There is a substance change afoot in the way we organize to get work done—networks will dominate hierarchies. We know at a macro level that creativity and value production come much more readily from free market economies than from centralized economies and the same thing is true for businesses. Collaborating with free market ecosystems will be key to competitiveness in the future. Key to your business is unleashing the free market potential—using the social mobile cloud to reorganize the way work is done and the role of leadership.

This may feel like old news. You already know the workplace is changing. But knowing and doing are two different things. How far have you taken the vision, the possibilities, in your mind and, more important, in your actions? How much have you broken down the hierarchical decision making and created processes that enable employees to band together dynamically to solve problems and make decisions?

Let's start with this vision: What will we do when we're all brainpower, not manual labor? The end of labor is coming—the elimination of muscle power as a part of the production process has been under way throughout the Industrial Era—more and more of the physical work can be automated and ultimately roboticized. The end of labor means abundance, with the option to work less and less. If we evolve society in a healthy way, abundance will mean that people will be provided for without them being productive in their own way. But the difference between having enough to eat and having wealth will be in how we use our brains.

Our future work environments will be all about information processing—from the simplest tasks where we are simply somewhat better than a computer to the most complex acts of creativity. Our systems of employment and reward will have to shift to reward these new models.

Business Model Shift 10: Dynamic Networked Social Sales and Support Staff

The idea of turning customers into sales agents has been exploited in many different guises over the years. But these sales models all depended on managing complex hierarchies, sometimes called multilevel marketing systems. Because the cost of communication and the corresponding cost of coordination were very high in the business environment in which these sales relationships were created, a great deal of oversight was necessary. Sales representatives had to be supervised, and that meant they also had to be evaluated and screened, allowing only the most successful to remain in the program.

Imagine the inefficiency of this model—if you were able to succeed in a sales associate role relatively quickly, you would be retained. But if your path to success took a few detours, you might be cut from the pool before you showed any sign of success. But what if in the long run that slow producer was actually a better salesperson than the individual who found a quick route to success? The organization would never discover this, building a suboptimal sales organization only because the system dynamics rewarded the quick salesperson and perhaps not the best salesperson.

The social mobile cloud provides a way for you to allow anyone to become a sales rep or a support rep and to reward them simply on the basis of their performance. Set the rules of the game—design the system to engage people—and let them evolve the models within the constraints you have set in order to achieve their own definition of success. And when cloud-based services can substitute for human supervision, do you care how many people have signed up to be sales or support staff? If one of them is not performing at some minimum effective level, is there a real cost to leaving them in the system when the management of their performance has been automated? And when their rewards are calibrated to their contributions?

Digital transformation leveraging the social mobile cloud will amplify positive results and reduce friction. It will allow you to maintain more marginal contributors but will also help your best producers achieve more. Getting the design right for this is about leveraging the topics we've been discussing—social mobile cloud technologies, virtual currencies, and gamification.

Do this right and you can develop a network-distributed marketing and support staff. Self-sustaining, self-motivating networks will overtake inbound and outbound call centers in time. Early experimenters have already shown that significantly higher quality sales and service, with higher employee morale, can be achieved through very flexible working conditions. Flexibility creates a coordination cost—but when you automate coordination, you can permit greater flexibility. This is the state change—in the Old World, flexibility was too expensive. In the New World, not being flexible will be too expensive!

One of the compelling things about an online, distributed, and mobile workforce environment is that the work itself can be tied to corporate sponsored currency and gamification. The concept of work changes when it is fun. It becomes more interesting, more fulfilling, and because of that, people will do a better job.

Imagine a world where everyone has a computer terminal where they can earn stored value and then buy products and services. People will work to earn value on their own schedules and according to their own needs—not on a fixed factory schedule. And the more capable people will do more to earn more of the stored value. People are acting this reality out right now in online games.

Political campaigns have experimented with these dynamic work models, partly because they rely so heavily on volunteers. A campaign's "get out the vote" effort, traditionally done through a combination of walking door-to-door and calling from expensive to operate temporary call centers, can be transformed by the social mobile cloud. While walking through a neighborhood is still important, the call center component changed dramatically by evolving into an organic and dynamic self-organizing model.

The traditional model is for a campaign to construct temporary call centers, staffed by volunteers, with specialized computer systems and phone banks designed to draw from a database of likely voters and with the computers automatically placing calls and connecting staff as they are ready to engage with the next person. But a new call center format has been emerging.

The first step is to adopt the consumerization of IT to circumvent the expense of temporary call center equipment—have volunteers bring your own device (BYOD). Instead of showing up and using specialized temporary call center technology, volunteers can be expected to show up with their own laptop computer and cell phone. The only thing needed in these temporary spaces is a WiFi connection to the Internet. Each volunteer can be handed a preprinted list of likely voters and asked to use their own phones to place the calls and to use their laptops to record results through a web interface to a central database.

This model can be improved on further by extending the simple Web form to allow anyone, anywhere to make a call to a likely voter—the Web form can display the next phone number in the queue and a volunteer—sitting anywhere—could dial that number, talk to the voter, and record a result on the Web. Campaigns are already successfully implementing completely distributed, virtual "get out the vote" campaigns in which anyone can participate.

Airlines have been among the first commercial entities to utilize the same idea with stay-at-home agents taking calls, allowing employees to work flexible schedules that fit into other responsibilities—perhaps providing care for elderly parents or children or making time for other interests. Letting people work from wherever and whenever gives a company access to a broader workforce, creates higher job satisfaction, reduces turnover, and as a result increases quality.

But the next iteration for commercial entities will extend to ad hoc work forces providing sales and support for companies. The models are already developing—many companies now have what is referred to as an affiliate model as a part of their online sales strategy. Anyone can act as an agent to send referrals to the company and if a purchase is made, the agent gets some small cut of the sale. There are people who make a living developing Web platforms that attract audiences and serve as gateways for multiple online retailers.

Similarly, customer support is increasingly available in online communities—customers helping other customers. In some of the most advanced online forums, companies reward their most helpful customers with recognition and monetary awards.

Designing systems to manage quality and properly recognize contributors is still complicated, but it will be increasingly prevalent as companies adopt dynamic networked workforces.

Business Model Shift 11: Workforce Collaboration to Improve Safety and Quality

Manufacturing, assembly, construction, and other blue-collar jobs are also about to be transformed and become information rich and collaboration intensive. In talking to the chief technology officer of a major industrial company, one of the key technology systems that the company is working to deploy is a wireless location sensor that allows management to instantaneously determine the location of every employee on a work site or plant. This is useful in the case of an emergency—whether employees all make it to safety areas or are still in dangerous areas is always a question in a crisis. But imagine the implications if this data were available in real time to all employees. I need a supervisor; which one is the closest to my location? I have a problem that I know Joe can solve; where is he in the plant right now?

Add to this the ability to use these devices as mobile environmental sensors, collecting and reporting data from around staff on a constant basis. Are dangerous fumes developing in a mine? Is the radioactivity level higher than expected in a nuclear power plant? Are chemicals leaking from machinery? The social mobile cloud makes every employee a passive or even an active node in a sensor network throughout any industrial environment.

Imagine the construction site where a worker can immediately snap a photo of a dangerous condition and transmit it to a collaborative group that might contain peers, union representatives, safety inspectors, and company supervisors. The photo is time stamped and has embedded geo-location data. The information about the incident is transparent to all participants and can be investigated and rectified immediately.

In a manufacturing environment, catching a product safety or quality problem before the product has left the factory has the potential of saving an enormous amount of money for a company that might otherwise have the direct and indirect reputational expense of a product recall.

Enabling employees to collaborate to improve safety and improve quality will be a core feature of the social mobile cloud.

Business Model Shift 12: Transparency and Openness

Ultimately, the power shift enabled by the social mobile cloud provides employees with the ability to participate in a wider range of decisions—and if leadership permits this kind of engagement, this change will help organizations. However, denying employees the opportunity to ask questions, understand the reasons for decisions, or even influence the outcomes will lead to dissatisfaction by employees—higher turnover, higher recruiting costs, less capable staff, and worse—rebellious employees who simply take their conversations into the commercial Internet where consumer tools are available to serve these purposes.

Let's go back to the idea of everyone being a CEO of their own lives. It makes sense that when a workplace that splinters into many parts, the remote workforce will start to resemble a smaller corporate entity. When you work remotely, you have to start thinking about the big picture in order to succeed, to start understanding not just your job but how it fits into the whole company you are serving. Independence means taking responsibility. Really let this key concept sink in. It's to your advantage. Whether employees are still captive but just becoming mobile, or if they're truly autonomous freelance consultants, everyone is now not just empowered but obligated to have an overarching knowledge of the company. And that is without you forcing them to do it, with varied attempts at ineffective training. The accumulation of knowledge is being driven by the workforce, and that is why it is working.

Fractalization of the workplace lends itself to accountability, job satisfaction, very high levels of collaboration, and positive financial results if you build the environment well. Remember to compete against yourself but to collaborate with others. This is true at each level of the fractalized workplace.

The First Results of the Fractalized Workforce

Before examining the front-running method for turning fractalization into long-lasting profit and well-being, here is a glimpse of some initial implications, the result of early fractal stages, borne from, you guessed it, placing a smartphone remote control in the hands of employees.

If you want a baseline barometer of the economy, take a look at how the behavior of blue collar workers is changing. Okay, so let's see how they're going fractal with smartphone remote controls.

Workers who work outside offices—construction sites, factories, transportation, pest control, appliance repair, and the delivery industry—are gaining a huge advantage from the remote control abilities of smartphones. They increasingly have the ability to be decentralized, communicate from the field and on the road, obviating the need to check in at a headquarters, which wastes time and fuel. They also can communicate directly with customers. The need for a dispatch operator, for instance, in the pest control, cable, satellite TV, or appliance industries, is forever gone. The technician coming to your house can call you from his smartphone to say he is on his way. He can order parts and schedule appointments from an app, cross-sell existing customers on new products and services. Remember the days not so long ago when the cable TV repairperson would call to say he was on his way, but you failed to answer the phone in time? There was no way to call him back. You would try to call dispatch, and they'd try in turn to reach the repair technician by sending a message, but it was all in vain. Without confirmation, he'd move on to the next call. You would have to reschedule. Now you can text him directly; there's no longer a middleman. The great untethering is changing where we work and the ways in which the work is structured.

What we're seeing is more autonomy altogether, incredible communication and collaboration capability. That is true for both blue collar and white collar workers. Every person is also the CEO of his or her personal brand. Even the cable TV repairperson.

Your employees have the same remote control smartphone that you have. Remember that. Your employees have the same access to the cloud as you have, which with its low cost and supremely global access, means removing barriers of entry to start businesses. Remember that too. And many of your employees, especially the younger ones have likely been avid participants in social networking for a lot longer than you have. Maybe remember that above all else. They have all started to adapt to the social mobile cloud. They are all hanging on, leading or following fast to avoid being thrown from the chain.

Perhaps you are starting to see where I'm going with this relationship shift. It amounts to a significant power shift between employee and employer. The employee is more powerful than ever before and gaining even more ground every day. And that power is being wielded with self-interest in mind. There is no such thing as the journeyman employee anymore. Take the company man out of the collective business glossary. Companies burned that bridge with employees long ago.

People don't always have to have a financial reward—a reward can be recognition, a great work environment, participating in a tremendous achievement, but you need to design into your system real rewards to attract the best and brightest. Even so, don't count on the best and brightest staying around forever. Why would they? Think freelance, think consultants. Give them great projects, reward them well, create a really fun work culture, and leave the door open for future collaboration. Remember that openness is the operating system for the social mobile cloud. If a star employee could easily become a competitor one day, make sure it is more appealing and safer for him or her to consult to you, or partner with you, or freelance for you.

There is a real benefit from thinking this way: When you reward based on merit, and design your company to embrace change, fresh ideas, and new people, your company will stay youthful, inspired, invigorated. That culture alone will entice great people, creating a corporate ecosystem of productivity and growth.

It is not as if you can stop the tide, or find a new way to guard crumbs. You can't. And the attitude of continually attempting to treat employees as prisoners will make everyone, including yourself, miserable. More important, the other companies in the knowledge economy will innovate around you and leave you behind, snapped off the end of the whip.

Results Not Rules

A new form of work, sometimes called the results-oriented work environment, will take off in the new mobile workforce as the result of fractalization. Everyone will have to ask: Why are we tethered to a desk when being in the field or in the factory will help get things done more efficiently? Why are we working 9 to 5 when the work could be done more efficiently from 12 to 8 since it involves talking to a team in Bangalore? Why am I at my desk in Waltham when I could be at a restaurant in Boston reviewing the video on my mobile and sending the approval to the creative team?

Caring about results rather than rules means that it isn't the modern version of the Industrial Age punching the clock that will bring a pay raise or a bonus. Employees are measured against tasks achieved and goals accomplished. Mobility accelerates this by giving us the ability to be connected anytime, anywhere.

Some people will read this and rebel: "I don't want to be accessible at all times! I don't want to work around the clock!" When mobility is done wrong, businesses risk burning out employees, making them less effective, not more. Flexibility to achieve results on your own schedule doesn't mean having no schedule. Instead, focusing on results must be about allowing employees to define work time to both suit their needs while also achieving the company's objectives. It can make those great employees and freelancers stay with your company longer. By the way, compensation will adjust as well to your ability and willingness to achieve these objectives.

This sometimes requires compromises. Connecting with a global workforce requires that we be willing to take a call earlier in the morning or later in the night than we'd normally be at work, but doing so should also create flexibility in the middle of the day to help out at our children's school or go for a swim.

Fractalization and a focus on results may be easy concepts to digest intellectually, but they can be very difficult to bring to life in any company, even organizations with positive, easily adaptable cultures. Don't become daunted. If you want to make changes but aren't sure how to set the policies in place, start small and think about how to evolve over time. The foundation for this change is to establish measurability for the tasks that people do in your organization—remember, measure everything!

How many days does it take to get a purchase order issued or a vendor paid? Track this, set goals for improvement, reward success. Roll an individual's tasks up into team goals, group goals, division goals, and show people how they connect. When does getting a purchase order turned around faster help a company bring a product to market more quickly? Show the person processing the forms how his or her role has a cascading impact through the organization.

Once you have started down this path, you will want to develop your own model for learning from data—analytics-driven dashboards that establish key results that connect with your organizational objectives. Every decision is by definition the irrevocable allocation of scarce resources—you improve your ability to make decisions when they are driven by data—and you create a better work environment for your fractalized workforce because they can see how what they do connects to results.

III

PART

Understanding Change:
How to Adapt to the Social Mobile Cloud

13

Understanding Change

Analysis of geological evidence suggests that a vast ice sheet covered much of the Northwestern United States and Western Canada 20,000 years ago. Called the Cordilleren Ice Sheet by geologists, it is thought to have covered two and half million square kilometers and melting water from this ice sheet is believed to have created an enormous body of water, Lake Missoula, held back by an ice dam at what is now the Clark Fork Valley. Studies of this area and the surrounding Columbia Gorge and Scablands suggest that periodic rupturing and rebuilding of the ice dam caused enormous floods—scouring out channels, moving boulders the size of buildings, digging out huge potholes, and reforming the landscape of Northern Oregon over the course of an estimated 40 individual flood events.

Imagine glacial Lake Missoula, and great blocks of ice floating on its waters. One day there is calm, smooth water on the lake. A light breeze from the west is warming the waters that are still being fed by the melting ice sheet to the north. The fresh cold water sinks to the bottom and the warmer water rises to the surface. Some of the floating ice has come together and slowly frozen together to make a dam, allowing the level of the lake to rise. However, the warmer surface waters are slowly undermining the ice dam. At some point, a huge section of the dam breaks free and the calm water becomes turbulent as millions of gallons of water are released from the lake. Anything floating near the dam will be carried over the top. A block of ice floating at a distance from the dam simply moves closer to the edge, and as the level of the water stabilizes, it returns to calmly floating on smooth water.

Punctuated Equilibrium

I just described a geological manifestation of punctuated equilibrium—periods of calm separated by moments of catastrophic change. Now imagine the world as we know it as the lake, and all of our beliefs and expectations about how we and our organizations function as the floating blocks of ice. During periods of calm, these beliefs float gently—they seem normal and stable. They might move or change in a gradual manner, but it is easy to believe that the world we live in is a calm and orderly place. But when a major change confronts us and there is a period of sudden shifts in our environment—the ice dam breaking—our beliefs are in turmoil. Some ideas must be modified, some rethought, and some of them will disappear altogether to be replaced with new ideas—different and challenging until we get used to them.

Just like the narrow gap leading out of the river valley that causes the dam to form by blocking the flow of water and ice, there are mechanisms in our society and our companies that block our ability to change—reduce our capacity to ADAPT—and instead of showing adaptability, our organizations and our beliefs can become obsolete. One of the difficult things to understand is how the gradual changes, such as the slowly warming waters on the surface of the lake, can contribute to the cataclysmic periods of change—how supposed equilibrium is really an illusion. Successfully navigating the turbulent waters of change is in part about preparing for the change by recognizing the currents of warm water that are bringing about change.

Take as an example the bookselling business, which seems to be increasingly superseded by both online book sales and ultimately electronic book sales. These two trends are the warm water into the lake of the book industry. Imagine a fictitious neighborhood in which five booksellers equally share in serving local demand for book purchases. As the warm waters erode local demand for books in favor of online and electronic sales, all five retailers grow weaker. At some point, one of the booksellers gives up and closes his shop (the dam breaks). While overall demand had been reduced, the remaining customers of the closed bookshop are now redistributed among the four other bookshops. For a while, those four shops actually see some improvement in their business as the customers of the fifth shop show up, looking like new customers to the remaining merchants. But the underlying forces are still at work and the market continues to shrink—eventually forcing one after another of the bookstores to close.

Another thing worth noting about this process is that it typically does not proceed at an even pace, but follows instead a curve that is slower at first, speeds up as the trends gain momentum, and then slows again as the change enters its final stages (and late adopter markets). At the same time, the old ways of doing business are declining in their usefulness, the new ways are following a similar pattern—slower to grow as only the early adopters embrace the new way, then speeding up as mainstream adoption occurs, and then finally slowing again as the late majority reluctantly joins the crowd. I call this the wings of change after the shape made by plotting the reversal in fortunes of old and new.

The most critical and most dangerous part of this process is within the middle region I have shaded in which the two trends cross—and also the period of rapid acceleration and success of the new and subsequent failure of the old. This is the period when individuals lose their jobs, companies go bankrupt, or governments are overthrown. It is also when careers are made, fortunes are earned, and new civilizations rise. And of course this diagram doesn't pretend to show the reality of any particular change—the road is bumpier than the smooth curves suggest.

Reinvention

The economist Joseph Schumpeter described this cusp period as *creative destruction*, a term later popularized by free-market economists to refer to the process by which companies reinvent themselves or are replaced by new companies in response to changes in their industries. Whether or not Schumpeter's own conclusion that capitalism's cycles of creative destruction will ultimately lead to its demise as a system is correct, the process can be seen playing out over and over again in different industries, triggered by competitive shifts in markets caused by, among other things, technological change, environmental change, globalization, or shifts in our population and civil societies. See Exhibit 13.1.

A popular theory outlining how a technology moves through different stages of adoption within a population explains how each group of adopters thinks about change in different ways. Different models have somewhat different designations for the groups, but they

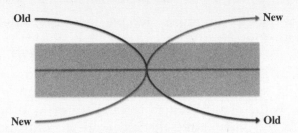

EXHIBIT 13.1   The Accelerating Decline of an Old Model Is Matched by an Accelerating Rise of a New Model

are generally clustered into three distinct groups: early, majority, and laggard. The early adopters have a very high tolerance for risk, and an interest in being opinion leaders. Each subsequent group contains members with a lower threshold for risk and lower interest in opinion leadership.

Going back to Lake Missoula, we can recognize the icebergs as laggards—waiting as long as possible until gravity pulls them over the edge of the breaking dam. Our willingness to recognize and embrace change can help us avoid being that ice.

This section is all about the adaptability that you and your company need to develop to survive and thrive as the pace of change continues to increase. How will you and your organization overcome the fear of failure and the fear of uncertainty? Why will you embrace a desire to change the world or at least a fear to miss great opportunities?

First, in Chapter 14, we will explore the problem of resistance to learning—why at a certain age there is a tendency to feel accomplished or experienced and to resist unlearning patterns that have helped us to achieve success up to that point. Then, in Chapter 15 and Chapter 16, we will explore new ways of working and thinking in *systems thinking,* which is a way of deconstructing and making sense of complexity and data-driven decision making that will be essential to overcoming intuitive, experience-based ways of operating.

CHAPTER 14

Undoing Our Resistance to Learning

There is a radical transformation under way in how our schools and classes are structured—increasingly focused on the premise of learning new ideas, big picture thinking and decision making, instead of on memorization or rote tasks, and recognizing that people's aptitudes cannot be classified based on a single mode of learning.

Part of understanding why we resist change is in understanding and therefore unlearning our bad learning habits. The hackneyed expression of being a lifelong learner will really take on new meaning in this century of constant change and the corresponding challenge to adapt.

Fundamental to overcoming a resistance to change is the ability to open yourself up to learning new things and in turn using your enhanced ideas, senses, and memory to facilitate that learning. Fear can be insistent, however, because we have been taught that there are right and wrong answers and that these answers are settled matters, not open to questioning. And to question a right answer is to open yourself to ridicule or worse. So fear tells you: Don't question. Don't challenge. Don't go against the grain.

But it is important to understand why that fear constantly steps in when you're about to embark on learning something new. Figuring out why we resist change, and in turn altering our operating premise when we are faced with the need to make changes, is the key to our personal success.

HIDE

There are four major reasons we resist change, which I like to call HIDE, short for habit, identity, defensiveness, and expectation:

1. **Habit.** This is our tendency to say it is okay the way it is; we're used to what we do, and it has been working. This is the voice that says if it is not broken, don't fix it. Part of the habit-driven resistance is also the way we convince ourselves that we like our way best even if we've never tried another way.
2. **Identity.** This is our tendency to make our resistance part of our identity, the way we see ourselves. This is a stubborn and detrimental sort of resistance, because we self-impose limits and labels.
3. **Defensiveness.** This is our tendency to say we're too good for a particular kind of change because that change insinuates that we're menial.
4. **Expectation.** We have an expectation that we will fail—and from this a tendency to be filled with fear. We have a legacy of negative reinforcement bestowed on us by our industrialized educational institutions, telling us (wrongly) what we can and can't do and telling us that we will fail if we wander too far from what we have been taught.

We can rid ourselves of the need to HIDE, literally and figuratively, by defining and making a mental note of the four reasons. That way, when we come up against our resistance, we can remind ourselves that the obstacles are emotional conditioning rather than capability, and in turn move on to exciting change.

Habits: They Make Us All Creatures

I particularly like the following definition of habit, "An acquired behavior pattern regularly followed until it has become almost involuntary."

I like it because we perceive that our habits give us control and safety, but the notion that a habit is an involuntary behavior means we have given up our control.

We all have places in our lives where we cling to our comfort zone, the sweet spot of our habits, even when we know somewhere deep inside that it is time to change. It is often funny to the outside observer. Consider people who still insist that they don't need to text on their cell phone, even if their job and personal lives are being highly compromised at this point without communicating in this way, and even if they already e-mail. But there are some people who won't budge and take pride in the fact that they won't budge. Why should they change? They act as if they would be thrown off their game if they start texting.

What is this phenomenon about? We all do it in some form: writers who still claim the typewriter or pen and paper is best for them, even if they've had manuscripts with no backup versions burn in accidental fires, become soaked in the rain, be trampled by the dog, or saturated in a coffee spill. And they pay people to transcribe their words because no publisher will accept typewritten, hardcopy work anymore. Or think about people who still buy expensive CDs instead of just the individual songs they want conveniently downloaded to their computer and music player, even if they also claim to be opposed to environmental waste.

When habit-driven resistance is present, it is always when a personal behavioral change is required for something that specifically makes life easier because the environment has changed—because technology has improved. It is always about an invention that is clearly making many other people happy and productive. And it is always about something we really need to do for work or social interactions, to keep up with our changing environment.

But despite all those positives, many people still think of changing as fixing something that is not broken. Part of our resistance is that we like getting used to things because it is comfortable. "Used to" is a tricky phrase, because while it denotes comfort on some level, it can also mean a rut because it closes us off to the possibility of liking new things as much as we like our old ways. Eventually, liking only the old means we stop growing.

As children, we don't decide we like one thing and then just stick with it. On the contrary, parents are constantly telling children that they said they wanted to try something, and they need to stick with it. But children are so open they'll take anything new and try it (except often for new foods, but that is a texture issue, which they grow out of). Children let a new thing replace what they thought they loved best five minutes ago. That is a great disposition. They know they can still love the old things, or at least the old ideas, but put their energy into new things as well. They do not see old and new as mutually exclusive, but rather as cumulative. They're not threatened.

As adults, we often let our habits define us. Interestingly, we are far more linear thinkers than children, yet we choose not to see the cumulative nature of learning new skills as change happens around us. The reason is that the problem is really all emotional.

Identity: Our Own Limits Cause the Inevitable Crisis

When we are children, parents and teachers start defining us by labeling us. For those of us with siblings, these remarks will ring a bell: He's the smart one, she's the social one. He's the athletic one, she's the mathematical and cautious one. He's very academic, she's the artistic one. What is inherent in these sorts of backhanded compliments is that while you have one set of strengths, other personality features are weak and insignificant. Figuratively, you can hear the doors slamming on confidence in weak areas.

If you are a child and the adults around you keep insisting you are one thing and therefore by definition not another, by the time you are an adult you will impose these limits on yourself. We all do it, and many of us, especially at family-of-origin gatherings, will even joke about it. But for adaptability it is not enough to understand why we limit our identities—that is essentially what we're doing when we joke about our shortcomings at family gatherings. We need to go a step further and undo the self-imposed limits.

What is so insidious about labeling children is that human beings learn different sorts of skills at different paces, so to label ourselves while bodies and brains are still growing is completely illogical. Think about one of the scientific reasons that the legal drinking age was raised to 21 years old in the United States. Studies showed that a teenage brain isn't fully developed enough to govern the loss of control or to have sound judgment. Yet, we label children's ability by age 9 in our public school system, more than a decade before their brains have formed enough to even start assessing strengths and weaknesses. A very athletic child may well turn out to be highly interested and capable intellectually, but his or her physical prowess simply developed first.

Think of how dangerous the adult manifestations of these identity limits are, in terms of the way we see ourselves in context of our environment: The writer mentioned earlier, with the pen and paper and monthly transcribing expenses, considers himself of a vintage character. Our egos will attach some perceived positive attributes to our identity limits; otherwise we would all be completely depressed. And being a vintage naturalist is very common, which is why I turn to this sort of example. There are other ones that are analogous, such as the artist who won't learn graphic design on the computer. This vintage attitude in particular is critical to address because it directly affects the person's ability to earn a living.

So the writer and the artist, in this case, have attached Luddite cache to their ways. And the Luddite cache is quite profound. Ned Ludd was an early nineteenth-century textile worker in England. From 1811 to 1816, Ludd organized bands of rebels to destroy new, state-of-the-art machinery brought to the textile manufacturing plant in Leicestershire, where he worked. The reason he was against mechanization? Ludd was certain it would mean a diminished number of jobs.

Two centuries later and nothing has changed emotionally. Yes, Ludd was correct in his concern. Technology replacing physical labor is a revolutionary change that is happening rapidly, and today's physical laborers must go through revolutionary personal changes to adapt to the new workforce. In a matter of two decades, the number of physical labor jobs, if it continues to follow current trends, will be drastically reduced, from about 50 percent to 10 percent of employment. People will have to learn to work with their minds instead of with their muscles. The good news is that learning to work with our minds has never been more accessible to the entire population. It is arguable that the mechanically inclined teen without means can readily learn to turn his aptitude into brainpower by accessing a tailored way of learning and spending as much time tinkering with computers as he would looking under the hood of a car.

New technology may take away certain jobs, menial unsatisfying ones, but it paves the way for new industries and a lot more, higher quality jobs for those who acquire new skills. When you can rely on your brain to make your living, rather than your muscles, your ability to make a living will also have a longer life span. Aging, injury, or simple fatigue and wear and tear on the body threaten blue-collar livelihoods and standards of living.

For those adept at physical labor, it may end up being the most interesting time of change, because they will end up more well-rounded, perhaps even inventive because they can physically prototype their ideas even before being able to generalize the work into something that is done by machines or robots. This is a path for the physical laborers who can be the artists of our era.

The key is overcoming our fear of change, and we'll get to understanding where all that horribly profound fear we suffer from collectively comes from in a moment. For now, consider a deeper look at the effects of attaching limiting identifiers to yourself.

If you ever want an instant cure to being a true Luddite, take a trip to England, and go see how even the wealthiest courtiers and monarchs lived 300 years ago. We'd consider the conditions worse than today's third world. In the United States, for the same experience, visit George Washington's house. Would you want to live like that? Seeing the big picture can help us see the need for little changes. And in many cases, little changes are all we need to do, in the grand scheme of things. In Chapter 15, I explain how to get to big picture thinking from here. Training yourself to think of the big picture helps remove the fear of making small, incremental changes, it empowers us, and, as a side benefit, it cures the stress we experience from information overload.

Perhaps the most important thing to remember when the environment changes and we therefore must change our ways: It doesn't mean you have to give up your belief system, or the love for the way you function, or your identity. You're simply adding something to it that helps you function, while you do what you love. You're simply being expansive, and expansive is youthful. It will keep you young, and happier.

The person who hasn't given over to texting instead of live conversation can try a new attitude:

> I don't have to like texting, but now my friends, peers at work, and my kids in some cases, find these varieties to be their primary mode of communication. If I want to stay connected to the people who prefer to write in real-time shorthand form, I will text with them. It doesn't take away from who I am, it simply adds a dimension, my ability to communicate.

Maybe understanding why some people love to text would help. Maybe some people are shy on the phone, and e-mail is too detached because it's asynchronous, so they're relieved to have texting, where they can express themselves better. This phenomenon, where something used to work perfectly well and then suddenly it's inadequate—talking live instead of texting—is often about new choices that have long been desperately needed but simply weren't available. The people who are shy or feel inarticulate on the phone have long suffered live phone conversation, but it never worked for them. The moment there was something that met their needs, they jumped at the chance to use it. And adaptability can be largely as enjoyable as finding personal solutions, if you have the right attitude. Personal change in our era is often about finding the proper learning tools for your needs, and in turn, a tailored method of expression.

If you hate texting, but a deaf person, or someone simply hard of hearing, came into your life, would you begrudge texting back and forth with this person as the primary mode of communication? Of course not! Think about how great an advancement texting has been for the hard of hearing. Perhaps no other single invention to date has leveled the playing field for this disability. You can literally communicate with a deaf person and have no idea that the person is deaf if he or she doesn't tell you.

The point of asking if you'd mind texting with a deaf person is to show that once we find another person's need legitimate, and stop taking the request to change as a personal attack, we stop resisting change. Texting became a phenomenon because many people found it so comfortable. You can speak to someone even if you're shy, or in the middle of noisy city traffic. A baby can be crying in the background, TV blaring, vacuum cleaner going, and texters are in a nice, quiet world.

Resistance is often about our own judgment and holding back respect for other people's way of doing things if it is different from our own. As parents, we can catch ourselves doing this all the time with our kids. Kids really are a great mirror to our own behavior, shortcomings and all. We often watch the way kids do something, criticize it, then make them stop, even if they are accomplishing the task they're supposed to be accomplishing.

A very intelligent, high level, 45-year-old network administrator, who happens to suffer from attention deficit disorder (ADD), told me that as a child, his parents would never let him watch TV while doing his homework. They had decided it was bad because it was entertaining and they worried what other people would think. Think about this. They immediately imposed a negative association with his entire identity.

But because of his restlessness, and his ADD, he found that watching TV while doing his homework helped, especially since he was often bored with his homework. He said if he was really bored and there was nothing else going on to take up part of his brain's attention, he could not get started on his homework. His parents would get angry that he'd been sitting there forever, that the homework was easy, and he was too smart to act this way so he must be misbehaving. But he actually couldn't focus. Once the TV was on and there was mild distraction, enough to entertain part of him, he could fly through the homework in a matter of minutes.

He figured this out on his own, meeting his own needs by using what was available in his environment, specifically technology, to solve his problem. Today, if he is in the middle of a mind-numbing administrative task, which he must do, like it or not, he keeps a social network open on his screen while working, to chat or read. He needs to accommodate his partial continuous interest in things. And there is nothing wrong with that. Some parents would go straight to medicating their kids before letting them work with music on, or while texting, or if they have to play a guitar while doing homework. Why, if the kids are getting the work done? They are meeting the demands of their environment using tools that meet their individual needs and that make them productive and happy.

Sometimes we judge based on our own fear of how we appear. And that is where we're trapped in our own emotional hypocrisy, judging what we like and what we believe not based on productivity, happiness, or any other personal achievement measure, but rather by how it may look to others.

One of the fascinating aspects of our changing world is that it often enables our idiosyncratic behavior to be accommodated. Our identity, in all of its true forms, is acceptable without having to fit into strict paradigms. We all have idiosyncrasies. It might help us to embrace those idiosyncrasies rather than revert to primitive mob mentality. The fact that our changing world accommodates them, while making demands on us, is a great thing. Today, if I am ADD and need to change screens midsentence to look at something distracting for a moment before I return to working, I can do it without anyone the wiser. I don't have to get up, walk around, distract or disrupt others. Or even if the ADD behavior is visible, it is accepted if we are using tools to keep us productive.

One of the greatest gifts of accepting change is that the return on investment is fast. When the person who refused to text, even though he needed to, starts to text, within a few weeks he won't remember how he could have possibly gotten along without texting. Think of the cell phone. A colleague I had to pick up at the airport encountered a problem in customs and was delayed. If he didn't have a cell phone, he wouldn't have been able to let me know and I wouldn't have been able to adjust his agenda (letting others know he had been delayed), which would have caused concern, disrupted the day, and wasted hours of many individuals' time. What did people do before cell phones? There are so many circumstances that question would apply to. The most important answer might be: It is a good thing we no longer have to find out.

And that is perhaps the most useful thing to tell yourself when it is time to change and you're resisting because you like the way you do things: Chances are you will look back in three months and wonder how you ever did it the old way.

Here is an important secret for overcoming self-imposed limits on identity: There's a saying about 90 days. People can have a perspective on life changes in 90 days, so give any change you make three months and then decide what you think about that change. But don't decide before.

Any new physical habit, such as a new exercise program or healthful diet, will take 90 days to have real effect. If you break off a relationship but are uncertain if you really want to end it, stay apart for 90 days and see how you feel, and don't trust your feelings before then because they could be fear or habit, instead of what you really want and need. The same relationship advice applies to a new job. Learning curves and adjusting to new interpersonal work relationships can take time. Don't decide you don't like a new job until you've been there for three months.

The point is that you can't see clearly until you've made a change, sat with that change, and then look back with a fresh perspective. There is a natural rhythm to 90 days.

And therein lies the ultimate exercise for trying something new. Try it for 90 days. See if you miss the old way at all, if it compromises you in any way, or if it is still you but easier, happier, better, more productive. See what enters into your life as a result of your behavioral change. And if after 90 days you still don't like it, stop doing it.

Defensiveness: Guarding Crumbs with Knee-jerk Reactions

We all guard our personal power, sometimes to our own detriment. Consider for a moment how the very sentiment of being "perfectly capable of change but resisting" makes you feel. Not think, but feel. What is your initial reaction when someone says to you: "Come on, this new way is better. You can do this, why do you insist on your old way if it's not as good?"

If it gets your rebellious, antiauthority hackles raised, you're not alone. If it makes you think that whatever is being asked of you is beneath you and insulting, you're not alone. We all do it, even though there is mob mentality in knee-jerk rebellion, as much as there is mob mentality about blindly following trends. The term *knee-jerk* comes from the way doctors test reflexes by hitting your knee with a little hammer. The problem with reflex is that it is the opposite of thoughtfulness. It is the response of an animal without opposable thumbs and the ability to reason.

One caveat in my plea to resist knee-jerk rebellion: Make no mistake; those hackle instincts are powerful, positive human spirit survival instincts when turned on the right problems at the right time. Personal power and boundaries are key to confidence. Doing things your own way, and finding your own individuality is a testimony to the human spirit, to ingenuity, and in turn to the type of thinking that leads to invention. It is also the check and balance system against mob mentality. (Often the way change is presented to us is as a threat. But we'll get to that in a moment. That is part of the third reason we resist change, negative reinforcement in learning.)

The problem with knee-jerk rebellion against change is that it is usually misplaced resistance and actually leads to stripping you of your individual power and not preserving that power. Think of the following example, which might happen any given day of the week in an office environment:

A manager comes up to an employee and tells the employee that from now on the weekly report of work accomplished must be done in a different format. The employee has to hand in a spreadsheet, rather than a narrative document. For each task, there needs to be a box with what the task is, and another box with a status update, a third box with who on the team is responsible for what. The employee bristles because she doesn't really know how to use spreadsheets, so she immediately assumes it will take more time and a learning curve to put out the report. The employee also postures that learning how to use a spreadsheet is beneath her, for someone secretarial to worry about.

But what that resistance is really about is the employee's fear of the learning curve as well as the fear that without the narrative, it won't seem like she is accomplishing much. It is simply not her way of doing things, so she thinks she won't have any control over her own process. Her first overall reaction: "This will be bad and I won't be good at it." (You can start to see how the individual elements of our propensity to HIDE are entwined. By the time we're being defensive, it's because of habits, a misguided sense of identity, and expectation of failure, which I'll elaborate on in a moment.)

What we all fail to realize in the moment we're asked to change is that the most empowering move is to master the new skill as quickly as possible, and then amp up the rebellious energy. In the example of the employee who now has to turn in spreadsheets of work accomplished, consider this: Once she has that spreadsheet creation down, which will happen quicker than she imagined, she will find a way to make herself appear even more productive. For instance, she can divide tasks into subtasks that have immediate pictorial presence. If she starts out from the disposition that she can use the new way to her advantage, that is exactly what will happen. The mere fact that her boss will be more receptive is a great start. Think of the texting example again. Like the shy person who is more comfortable texting, maybe the boss reads slowly and has poor reading comprehension. If that boss is put at ease by a chart, then it is to the employee's advantage to give him or her a chart.

If someone has the ability to use narrative to her advantage, she'll be able to do a spreadsheet even better and present that compelling argument in a way that is appealing to those with less attention span. By zooming out and looking at the big picture of what is going on, taking into consideration everyone's point of view in the situation, and having the faith that spreadsheets are widely used because anyone can learn them, the employee will gain power (this is explained at length in Chapter 15).

If there is a relevant example in your own work life—and I'll bet there is—try changing your attitude first, then the actual way you're doing something. Think of the boss' request to change as an indication of their own strengths and weaknesses, rather than as a comment about you or a judgment of your worth.

The point is that any new format will offer its own advantages if you're open to learning it. If nothing else, the change might be fun.

Anything you've been doing forever means it has created a rut. Imagine only that the new way will take less of your time.

Remember that rebellion to the sort of change that is non-negotiable is cutting off your nose to spite your face. Adapting is not serving any authority. It does not render you subservient to any human. On the contrary, it is empowering because it means adapting to the environment, not unlike building shelter to stay out of the rain, or stopping global warming by not polluting. Intelligent people don't expect the environment to adapt to them, they adapt to the environment. If not, you harm the environment and ultimately yourself.

You will find your individuality and personal power once you adapt. So that is the place to start. Know that you're not giving in by changing, you're being in harmony with your surroundings. And that leads us to the second factor of resisting change: Fear of being able to learn new things. In the case of that employee, don't underestimate her fear of learning how to use spreadsheets and thinking she'll never be as adept with it as she was with the written word.

Expectation of Failure: Why We Are So Fearful

Perhaps the single greatest benefit to becoming adaptable is freeing ourselves from the shackles of perennial fear. Unfortunately, we live in a fearmongering society, and none of us is impervious to its automated negative effects, not the least of which is the fear of learning new things. We're afraid we'll fail and have to face our limitations. If we resist, we can simply say we never tried.

But that is not to say that we can't overcome our fears. We can! We just need to understand how we're terrorized, why, and how we doubt ourselves as a result. Once we demystify, we can dispel.

We can choose to learn in different, tailored ways. If the learning is tailored, we can learn absolutely anything. The most important aspect of adopting a new approach to learning is to cast off the negativity, fear, and expectation that you'll fail. It is up to us to change the way we feel about learning new skills, and the first step in that is to remove the fear. We can.

Your intellect is a given. Think of it as a large empty toolbox in your mind. Knowledge is simply material—tools—you gather to fill that box. You can attain any knowledge you want. And in terms of the best way for you to learn something? Consider that each tool box might have a different lock. You just need to find the proper key. Are you a visual learner? Tactile? There are ways to find this out, if you don't already know. And if you do know, for instance, that you are a tactile learner but you're trying to learn a new skill where hands-on teaching isn't immediately available, don't despair. There are tools now that can offer you a tactile experience when you need it.

Perhaps the most important aspect of learning new skills is to be open and assertive in terms of what you need in order to learn something efficiently and comfortably. There is no shame in needing tools. And new dynamic tools are here! It is the twenty-first century.

The key is to start by asking questions and knowing that there are no stupid ones. You will discover that there are many more avenues to find answers, and to do so with immediacy. The same behavior that locked you into fixed perspectives can open you to a new questioning. Gradual exposure breeds comfort, comfort breeds confidence, and confidence breeds focus end results. So gradually expose yourself to a posture of questioning rather than accepting!

The first question you may want to ask yourself is what new things do you need to learn. Make a list—think about how you envision yourself understanding them if there were limitless possibilities: Is it best if someone walks you through a process, do you like to read about a new topic first, with visual tutorials? Once you think about what you need, you can start the process of finding the tools you need. If you have a smartphone, you can find out easily, using your sense of digital kinesthesia to jump in and research our global network of tools and ideas, and get social feedback while you're at it, join a community of people just like you.

Start by searching for apps in the education category on your smartphone. Here is a list of app categories on smartphones: games, entertainment, utilities, social networking, music, productivity, lifestyle, reference, travel, sports, navigation, health care and fitness, photography, finance, business, education, weather, nooks, medical. There is an entire world and roadmap to learning, right there. Just click and get started.

Trains, Phones, Record Players: The Cause of *What*?

If you encounter self-doubt along the way, that the newness you're experiencing is somehow false and wasting your time, take a look, just for comic relief, at a few examples of attacks on technology that seem idiotic now. Guess, for instance, which technologies people thought would cause death and illiteracy? Trains, telephones, and phonographs.

Time gives us perspective, and like the discussion on memory, there is nothing quite so illuminating as perspective. Notice that the attacks were all fear-based:

- **Railroad travel.** Roughly two centuries ago in England the beginning of the modern railroad system was invented, fueled by the earlier invention of the steam engine. By the time the railroad concept made its way to the United States, the idea of speed, not just ease of travel with heavy loads, was part of the package. But many people actually resisted the railroads, saying that such travel could never work. It was the very notion that people could travel at more than 40 miles an hour that caused great alarm. And not even among laymen. It was scientists of the early 1800s who argued that the bones of human beings would be crushed by traveling at such speeds.
- **Telephone and phonograph.** Both the introduction of the telephone and the phonograph were met by people saying they were terrible inventions. There was real fear that people would never leave their homes and that recordings meant people would stop learning how to read.

The Crucial Skills for Twenty-First-Century Success

We are just learning how to teach the crucial skills for success in the twenty-first century: creativity and collaboration. We are all capable of learning—sometimes different things at different paces—and we need intellectual stimulation in different forms to succeed in the creative, idea-driven occupations, which will be the most important (and most highly compensated) jobs in the twenty-first century.

Many educational institutions are starting to develop new learning models and new tools. These new tools, approaches, and methods will ultimately change institutional learning but in the meantime they are making these resources accessible to any of us with a few clicks on the Internet. We just need to be curious and to explore.

Think about a child's curiosity and self-directed attitude and reapply that attitude. Keeping that sense of curiosity will help us keep learning. And children adapt so well because they don't have preconceived ideas about how learning should happen.

Even before access to the Internet became widespread, use of computers in education had been shown to shift the relationship between teacher and student to become more collaborative. Directly measured positive results include increased student motivation and self-esteem, increased technical skills, accomplishment of more complex tasks, more collaboration with peers, increased use of outside resources, and improved design skills and attention to audience.

Where our children are discovering these new tools and using them as part of their educational and social environment, those of us that left college before computers and the Internet became ubiquitous will have to relearn how to learn.

Continuous Learning: You're Either Growing or Shrinking

One of the most pernicious things that happens to us as we grow older is that we become good at some things—tasks, areas of knowledge, professions—and we cease to learn about other things. I say this is pernicious because while it can convey self-confidence and increase our net worth, it also reduces our perceived rewards for learning something new. And yet to be successful in a rapidly changing world, we need to be willing and able to learn new things continuously.

An employee at one of the companies I work with complained about being asked to learn how to use a new piece of software. She said it was a task for someone being paid far less than she was being paid. (Once again, identity in HIDE rears its head.) This comment exposes a genuine economic pressure against learning new things: If we are rewarded highly for one type of activity, we will tend to avoid activities that do not reward us as much. And we will look to task others with these activities rather than learning them. And we will in turn have less of an understanding for everything with which they are connected.

But another factor is also very important in her reaction. Being asked to learn this new tool was challenging and afforded the opportunity for this otherwise very accomplished professional to feel unaccomplished (expecting to fail in HIDE). Suddenly she felt like a novice in a world that she thought she had mastered.

When looking at statistics for Internet usage of all kinds, age clearly stands out as the most indicative attribute of those lagging behind in adoption and comfort with new Internet tools. One explanation for the reticence to engage online is that people age

45 and older tend to be at high levels in their careers, so they have less incentive to learn new skills. People who have mastered positions in their careers, but find those positions becoming obsolete, must join the fray, even if they perceive that that is beneath them.

Perhaps leisure time in retirement will increase engagement—time to play with new technology and the motivation to keep in touch with children or grandchildren. There is no ego involved in adapting for that reason. It is different from convincing people in the workplace to change.

A common refrain I hear from that group we earlier called laggards is that they don't have time or that they don't see the point of using these technologies. Whether it is a new cell phone feature, a social network, or learning how to record and edit audio or video, these people could be significantly enhancing their professional status, improving their business performance, and increasing their personal satisfaction at the work they are doing if they would only take the time to learn these new tools. If you find yourself saying you don't have time, or don't see the point, maybe look a little deeper, and just consider that it might be fear, and the need to HIDE.

One of the recurring behaviors I see otherwise accomplished people exhibiting in work environments is to ask others for assistance, rather than taking the time to learn something new. And they're not asking for help in learning the new task. They're passing the buck. I've mentioned this before, but I'm repeating it here because as we move on and really look at the tools we want to use to learn, I feel the need to emphasize that we all have the ability to learn. A common misconception of people over a certain age is that they assume they don't have the ability to learn. These are the people who will tell you things such as: If you don't learn a foreign language as a child, forget it, fluency will never be engrained. While it might be true that it takes more effort to become fluent in a language once you are past the age of 13, it is by no means true that fluency is out of reach.

And yet while virtually everything we want to know is a just few keystrokes away, we were raised in a learning environment in which experts (teachers) existed to be our guides. We expect someone to come along and teach. Worse, we often feel that we don't need to learn because we are already experts at what we do and we expect someone else to come along and do the new thing.

Meanwhile, those who have adapted to the new information rich environment become the teachers simply because they know how to use a search engine. This is not to diminish the value of asking for help, and indeed an increasing number of facilities are available online that make it easy to connect with experts. But the best questions are asked once the student has already gone as far as he can go on his own. The educational process is, in a sense, turned upside down online: Self-study precedes assistance from a teacher. Another benefit of self-directed learning is the stake the student has in the process. It is never about someone else's agenda. Let's take that notion to the workplace: Any time employees have a stake in the business, they perform better.

This is precisely why people start using the tools available if they are self-teaching, thereby getting a really well rounded, new economy education. They'll start searching online, and when they get stuck, they search out blogs and forums to find people with experience in the subject matter. And the online educational process provides a variety of points of view, teaching us to be discerning and analytical, as well as remembering that all authoritative bodies represent a point of view, not über knowledge. That, in turn, reminds us that simply absorbing and parroting back data is not real learning, or thinking. The online process of acquiring knowledge encourages us to think originally, because we must bring our own ideas to the table to synthesize the information we find online. No one opinion should ever overtake your thinking or be an overwhelming influence. When you embrace that idea, you will find your confidence soars. When you trust yourself, your imagination and curiosity start to come out to play. And that is when you will start to truly enjoy yourself. Learning new things, adapting to new ways, might in and of itself become your hobby.

So far we have discussed why things are the way they are, and why you needn't feel trapped or limited in your capacity to adapt and reap the benefits of the technological revolution. Now we'll put some of that capacity into action.

CHAPTER 15

Systems Thinking

A human chess machine is arguably the definition of an exemplary systems thinker. A systems thinker sees the big picture, doesn't get bogged down with minutiae, is extremely adaptable, and is open to learning by definition. A systems thinker is the sort of person who makes great life decisions because the future has been factored in, and the path to the best possible outcome has been analyzed and planned for. So what is involved in becoming a systems thinker, and why do chess players have this ability? Perhaps, more important, can you acquire this disposition even if you aren't a good chess player?

The answer to the latter is yes, but analyzing a chess player's point of view can help you adopt an analogous disposition.

Looking at the Whole

The key is that great chess players don't look at individual chess pieces, they look at the whole board. Using a technique cognitive psychologists call *chunking*, they see pieces in groups, perceive patterns in the relationships of these groups, and then make their moves (decisions) based on these patterns. Using this approach, they are able to solve a complex information processing problem in their heads that even the most powerful computer systems have trouble solving. The number of possible board arrangements and the multiplicity of possible moves is practically beyond comprehension. Success depends on transforming the problem from one of almost infinite possible moves to the best possible move based on recognized patterns.

In essence, this is using systems thinking for superior decision making. Each chess move is a metaphor for making decisions. Seeing patterns, thinking the patterns through while understanding that there is a beginning, a middle, and an endgame, and keeping your eye on the endgame at all times (you never hit a target unless you stay aimed on it) is how you play chess, and it is the quintessential example of systems thinking. Chess is a classic archetype of the game of life, the game of war, the historic obsession of mathematicians and army generals because it is so completely and perfectly metaphoric. With each move, the immediate possible next moves are changed even though the larger system of the game is still in place.

In this chapter and Chapter 16, I will discuss the synergistic relationship between this sort of big picture analytical thinking and a different approach to making decisions, an approach that will benefit you because you will base your (or your company's) actions on choosing the best possible move for any situation while keeping the big picture in mind.

I will often speak of these two activities together because of their cause-and-effect relationship. You can't have (good) decision making without systems thinking, and the whole purpose of systems thinking is better decision making. Furthermore, systems thinking doesn't happen and then a time lapse later you make a decision. Eventually, you understand that you use systems thinking to make decisions on the fly, and decisions are made every few minutes, with the big picture always in mind, the implications always thought through—just like chess moves.

In order to do that, you need not only to understand your immediate situation but what the situation will evolve into given the following: the consequences of each possible decision, the momentum and particular dynamics of the environment itself, and other people. That is chess. That is your job. That is your relationship with other people. That is any and every element of your life in the big picture. This is the sort of tactical thinking that is commonly known as seeing the forest instead of the trees.

Now what about those details? Herein lies the conundrum of the twenty-first century. Even the best general in an army can't forget the individual soldier for the sake of a troop mission. He makes the troop decision that will further the goals of the mission while protecting those soldiers. Without the soldiers, there is no troop.

You need to have details under your belt to have them factor in to the best big picture thinking and maneuvering. And there are far too many details now for you to have them all in your head, available to be analyzed on demand. You will not be able to cross the threshold of adaptability without the commitment to trusting technological tools to hold the details for you. You cannot systems think when you operate on information overload. If at this point you still feel resistant to tools like a smartphone and services in the cloud, look at your own life, where you're the civilian general: You have two kids and their team sports and homework, a demanding job, and a bear of a daily commute, and you still need to grocery shop and make meals and deal with economic constraints and keep your life organized and deal with crises at work and at home. That list doesn't even include friends, relatives, appliances that break down, cars that need repair, or medical issues.

There is more. Given all of that, what happens when someone asks you: Where do you see yourself in 1 year, 3 years, 5 years, 10 years? If 10 years from now is your endgame for career building purposes, what are your goals and what are you doing today to get there? (Answering these questions and planning a strategy is a key set of activities that you should embrace.)

You may laugh and respond that even with the proper tools, today you'd be satisfied if you made it to the evening without any major breakdown in the system: You're easy, have matching socks on, and no one you know getting sick or injured or fired would do. You may respond that where would you possibly find the time to have goals, much less make steps toward achieving them?

This is where everything we've talked about so far can come into play. Imagine using technology like the smartphone to enhance your memory through instant access to the world's collective knowledge—so that you can learn anything you'd like to know in a relatively short period of time. Imagine your senses enhanced so that you can access information about your environment, including what defines your environment, in real time.

Wait, the problem just mushroomed, didn't it? It seems worse, not better. You can get even more information. Suddenly you have the problem of the expert chess player: enormous quantities of information that must be evaluated to calculate the best move.

In the end, this book is all about change, and so naturally the first thing I will suggest that you do, in order to get to clear systems thinking, is to change the way you look at this information: Look at large patterns first, and goals, with the assumption that there are details that will work in your favor to get there. You must start really knowing, not just believing, that your goals are possible. Then when you access the data, you will have a laser beam of focus, which will, in turn, help you to access the data that will support you, without running into too much extraneous data.

And remember, even running into some extraneous data, or data that contradicts the likelihood of the outcome you're gunning for, it will still feel manageable if that data is external to you, on-demand. So even if you need to adjust your course, or your company's course a bit to get to your end goal you will still get there. If one path toward that goal turns out not to be plausible, you don't simply say, it won't work, I have to give up on the idea. Instead the answer is: I need a new strategy to ensure that I get there. And then, you devise that strategy.

Shifts in Focus

It is in this offloading and focus shifting process that we discover what the chess master already knows—that there is knowledge in the aggregate that does not exist in any of the individual pieces of information. Overarching knowledge gives us what we all want most: choices.

As Aristotle said, the whole is greater than the sum of its parts. We've all had this experience. Sit in a group and brainstorm to solve a problem. You will come up with ideas that won't arise if each individual makes a private list of ideas to solve the problem. There is an even simpler example: When you cook, you put all the ingredients out on the counter. You can taste each ingredient sequentially, and each will give you a certain amount of information, a certain flavor. If you make soup out of these ingredients, its flavor will include all of the flavors but also have a substantially different additional flavor from the reaction of the flavors together.

Take a moment to understand how behavior changes when you can unload the details, use tools such as the smartphone and new tools that are developing, and frame the way you perceive systems thinking in an optimal way. If you simply use the tools without awareness of what is happening to your thinking, the real shift in focus from burdensome details to big picture thinking may take place, as your habits change, but it won't be intentionally. When you have intention, the focus not only shifts more efficiently, it shifts more profoundly because you become proactive, which is essentially optimizing the cause-effect relationship between systems thinking and decision making.

For example, if you have intention, you won't just notice all the cool things a smartphone does, and organize your phone in a pleasing way, you will start to organize your smartphone tool to accommodate the details you need, given the big picture (goals) you have established. You will have awareness when you are looking at the big picture, so you will see patterns and their implications faster and more intricately. In turn, you may automate tools to gather details you may need at a later time. These tools can be configured to be on the lookout for certain data, and store it and organize it when discovered. Over time, these details add up, generating patterns and implications, and contribute to the creation of the big picture.

Again, practicing systems thinking is like chess. You train yourself how to play chess. We also have to train ourselves to systems think. And we start that by understanding what is coming—aside from smarter and smarter phones and personal data banks in personal clouds—to enable systems thinking; tools we already have that not only amass and store detail, but also automate pattern recognition. It will help you understand that your goals in big picture thinking are completely within reach, in case you're worried that your pattern recognition capabilities might not be at a chess master level.

Tools to Assist with Optimizing Details

There is information in every aspect of our environment and in everything that we do. In the late 1990s, a group of scientists, entrepreneurs, and investors began to define what they called *ambient intelligence*—the way in which information would be collected by pervasive sensor networks, transmitted over computer networks, and then stored, analyzed, and presented through a variety of analytical systems, sometimes called information lenses.

The analytical capabilities that they envisioned would help us comprehend the massive amounts of information coming in from these sensor networks to support decision-making processes and in some cases support autonomous systems. Over the past decade, these ideas have guided the development of capabilities that we now take for granted.

A simple example already in use in many places is the roadway information systems that transmit data about how fast traffic is moving on the roads around us. This information, transmitted instantaneously to computers that can overlay traffic speed on maps and compute various routes, is already changing the driving habits of millions of people every day. By informing people in real time of a traffic problem ahead and giving them alternate routes, the information gathered in the environment is refined down to a decision that individuals can make about how they will get to their destinations. In a broad way this is how decision support systems will be integrated into everything we do in the future.

To return for a moment to the example of the chess master, the overlay of traffic data onto a map provides a computational support that makes us all into traffic masters. Imagine having to take in all of the individual data elements, the speed of every car passing every sensor. We would somehow have to chunk these data elements and then perceive patterns in them. But a computer system that aggregates the data for us and then overlays it onto a useful model for perceiving patterns (in this case a map) allows us to understand the traffic without being an expert. Just as in previous chapters where we explored how the application of technology could enable us to do something that our natural abilities would not allow, so too will computation facilitate our ability to comprehend all of this data.

Imagine your companies accumulated market information when this is widely available. Say you set up a three-year goal to achieve a certain market share for a new product. You could, for instance, have an analytical application—which might look like the traffic map icon on your smartphone—to factor in breaking news about competitors and then show you how it changes the overall view of that market. So, for example, if news breaks that people have been laid off, or a new president with new business goals has been hired, you would be alerted with a visual and narrative representation of the new landscape. Nothing is quite as effective as a visual to see the big picture. Think about the phrase big picture itself; it suggests that there is a visual of the landscape.

People laid off at your competitor might mean the opportunity overall looks less desirable for all the products in this category including your own. But it also might mean that your competitor has an unrelated problem, making it a good time to drive for market share gains. Maybe you'd literally see, in a 3D picture, the dimension of the competitive landscape and real-time data impacting different aspects, helping you to make a better decision about when to make your next move.

Interactive Data Visualization

Just like in the traffic and company information scenarios, here are the basics of how data visualization technology works: It is a process of compactly representing information in a symbolic language. Computers can help us create a rich visual experience around data by employing animated symbols that change their colors, sizes, shapes, and positions. Reducing information to visual symbols is core to how people have made sense of the environment throughout history, and the computer is just one new tool to help us do this efficiently and now with much larger amounts of information.

Consider for example the lowly arrow. While we take this visual indicator of direction for granted, it was only first used in 1737 for this purpose. In ancient times, the arrow was associated with weapons (or sometimes masculinity). However, with the medieval development of the compass (in the 1400s), the arrow began to develop its modern association with direction. Some of its earliest uses were in engineering diagrams and of course in maps. This latter use in maps and roads, the one that we take for granted and even think of as natural, only came into broad use in the twentieth century.

Today, as one example, TV stations used computers to animate fleets of arrows in motion to indicate the relative strength and direction of weather patterns interacting over a regional map. Through this, they can communicate a better understanding of what would otherwise be complex and hard to comprehend atmospheric data. Or as another example, arrows might be animated to illustrate the movements of vehicles in an accident, helping a jury understand what happened in complex multiple vehicle incidents.

These common applications are just early indicators for what is to come. Used properly, interactive data visualization is one of the most powerful tools we have available for making sense of large quantities of information. And new products are rapidly emerging to analyze and present a wide range of information, not just numerical data.

In one innovative project, a set of tools was created that allows individuals to explore statistical data about health, population, and economics in regions around the world. A website provides a user interface to a massive collection of data that can be explored by anyone with a connection to the Internet. Dynamic animations of complex data illustrate complex issues in a way that would otherwise take significantly more time and expertise to comprehend. For example, look at the relationship of health and education in 25 countries over the past 100 years—a complex problem solved easily by modern visualization technology.

Going beyond numerical data, a growing number of projects are exploring how to allow a user to sort and display visual information that has been categorized in different ways. In one demonstration, a researcher was able to interact in real time with the kind of info-graphic we are used to seeing in a newspaper, in this case related to the covers of a sports magazine. How many of these covers featured cyclists? How many featured football? Which sports were featured most frequently at certain times of the year? If you bring any kind of categorized data into this system, it allows you to quickly shift perspectives from one view to another and combine different kinds of categories to create new displays. These interactive tools create the opportunity to make new discoveries and insights about information.

The most important use for this interactive information is to inform decision making. Whether it is a businessperson, a policy maker, or anyone deciding on the best route home through traffic, we all need information to make decisions. And consuming that information through an analytical model and visualization tools will be essential to making sense of the large quantities of information we must comprehend.

Steps to Systems Thinking

Being a good systems thinker begins with the end in mind. What is your personal objective? What is your company trying to achieve? If you have clarity of your end goal, everything else will be easier. By having clarity of the outcomes, the middle game and opening will be more easily understood. First, you'll know what information to be looking for to understand those earlier steps in the game. Second, you'll have an analytical model to make sense of the information in the context of your end goal.

Once you have clarity of your ending point, success will lie in defining the information you need to make decisions, the technology used to collect and analyze this information, the tools used to display the results of this analysis, and ultimately in how you make the step-by-step decisions based on that information that take you move by move toward your goal. The best goals, information, and analysis are nothing if you don't then use them to make good decisions.

16

CHAPTER

Decision Making

What is a decision and why are we often afraid of making one? A decision is an irrevocable commitment of limited resources. So it stands to reason that we'd be afraid of making the wrong decision, even if we are using systems thinking to make the best possible decisions at every turn. We all know there are no 100 percent guaranteed outcomes, so it comes down to our comfort level with taking risk.

SAFE

Recall the HIDE model from Chapter 13 once more—the idea of taking risks, and which kinds of risks, is a big part of our habits, identity, defensiveness, and expectations. But we need to make decisions in life, no matter what. And we know they may as well be the best decisions possible, which often entails taking some sort of risk. In turn, we also know we need to take risks to get anything we really want or need. As a balance to HIDE, I will introduce one last model, which I like to call SAFE, to be used during any decision-making process. It is composed of these four components:

1. **Spend.** You have to spend resources no matter what, so as much as possible, minimize your commitment of resources for any decision. But remember that you can only minimize the commitment of resources to the extent that we can still execute the best decision possible. Spend is about the need to spend, but the goal of limiting it to the smallest amount (and shortest

time) in order to validate your hypothesis, support the decision, and achieve the goal.

2. **Act.** Nothing says risk like taking an action. But often a decision made too late is worse than no decision at all. Remember that the conditions are changing all the time—as if your opponent on the chessboard was still making moves regardless of whether you do or not. So make sure you are in the game.

3. **Foundation.** You are not taking actions at random or in a vacuum. To assess what is the best decision possible, and how much risk is appropriate, we must analyze the details and situation from a systems thinking approach, and combine that analysis with our intuitive assessment. Our intuition should always be questioned, however, and as quickly as possible replaced with data and analysis. Lack of data should not prevent taking action, but taking action should generate data—adding to a foundation for future decision making.

4. **Evolve.** In order to spend the right amount of resources, act at the right time, and build a foundation for future decisions, you need a method for collecting and processing all this information. That includes your own personal skills and also the technology that you and your organization develop to support decision making. You will never be finished with this task—developing your skills and tools will require ongoing evolution.

Perhaps your first reaction to this SAFE approach is that it is just another catchy phrase. I've introduced three such phrases in this book—first ADAPT and then HIDE and now a third. What is the purpose of these mnemonics? Are they just clever or do they serve a purpose?

The essential question for you to answer is in how committed you are to changing yourself. Providing the mnemonics should help you to question yourself in the midst of decision-making situations. We are always the most comfortable doing things the way we have always done them—most likely making decisions through intuition and experience, even if applying big picture systems thinking to a degree. But intuition can get you into trouble. It is critical to also find the right data needed to analyze the situation and question your intuition and experience. By providing these models, I hope to help you stop and ask:

Where am I (or your organization) on the ADAPT evolution with respect to the decision being made? Aware? In denial? Accepting, making progress, or truly evolving? Don't get stuck in denial and HIDE even if you aren't ready to make progress or evolve.

How are your habits, identity, defensiveness, and expectations playing into this decision, even unintentionally? Is your personal tendency to HIDE getting in the way of making the best decision? Obscuring or affecting how you are interpreting the data? Does every piece of information you have say yes but your gut instinct says no and so you still lean toward no? How can you overcome this but still remain SAFE?

What is the best decision to make? Recognizing that you must spend, but that you can limit what you spend to the least amount possible to achieve your objective, you need a model to make those irrevocable commitments of limited resources. To be SAFE, you must spend the right amount of resources (as little as possible to achieve your goals), act at the right time, and in doing so make sure that you are building the foundation for better decisions in the future and evolving your skills and tools. By doing this you will make better and better decisions over time.

Committing to Adapting

In order to *evolve* your skills and tools you'll start with a commitment to adapting and a recognition of the barriers that your instinct to hide (and those of your colleagues) will put up. The mnemonics are a part of the tools—they can give you the grounding to ask the right questions as you proceed in this journey. While I am introducing these ideas to help you understand how to adapt to the changing environment brought about by the technology of the social mobile cloud, you can also use them the next time you have a personal decision, or a decision at work—the change that you seek to bring about rather than a change to which you are reacting.

Say your goal is to get a particular job, for which you think you will need an advanced degree. Check your awareness—you have an idea of what the job entails, you think you know what it will take to get it, but are you sure? Do you have data? Go online and start researching what sort of education people who are doing just that have.

After you do some initial research on your own, consult people. Processing in a collaborative way is always helpful. And it is the beginning of fusing intuition with analysis. First, consult professionals in that field; find a mentor. That mentor might be a group of people online. It might be a person with whom you sit face to face. Find out the realities of advertising from professionals in the field. But also consult with a close friend who knows you well on a personal level.

After you gather more perspective, move on to analysis. Go back and do more research, this time in practical terms. What will it cost in money and time? How many jobs are there in this field? Is that number shrinking or growing? What skills do the most successful people have? It is important to analyze data in the context of the real world. And do not get caught in the denial stage by your tendency to HIDE—as you do this research, don't become overwhelmed or despairing of achieving your goal.

Plug all the information you gather into a 1-, 2-, 3-, 5-, and 10-year plan and see how it fits. The purpose of creating these plans is that often decision making depends on timing, so having short- and long-term options is helpful. The other benefit of these temporal plans is that it gives you a structure to test out decisions and risks in smaller chunks, and then expand those risks over time. For example, in the advanced degree example: Let's say that within the one-year plan is the plan to take your first classes in the field. Perhaps you'll take a degree requirement that is directly applicable to your job now, so if you don't like the long-term plan after all, you haven't wasted your time. The class you end up taking will help you in your current job.

In the same vein, if you find you really love the class, then your next decision will be to expand on your risk. You may reevaluate your two-year plan after the first year and add three more classes in year two, instead of two you may have initially planned for. This is called iterative decision making, which minimizes risk and maximizes benefit.

You will need to evolve your plan as you learn more. When you have a first draft of a plan, show or explain it to a mentor. There may be ways to commit fewer resources or minimize risk a bit more. You may also be able to achieve your goals through paths that weren't obvious in your first analysis. Be sure to use all the tools available and gain access to as much information as possible in an efficient way. That way you'll be able to proceed safely, spending the right amount of resources, acting at the right time, building your foundation, and evolving your skills and tools.

The same process applies equally well to a decision in your company as it does to this personal example. Imagine launching a product, expanding into a new market, changing the way you do marketing or customer service (or responding to the social mobile cloud)—how do you begin the process? How best do you evolve your (and your organization's) thinking so that you are making the right decisions? It may seem basic, but too often people don't start with the endgame. The new product competes with X, Y, and Z which currently makes up $100 million of a larger $1 billion market. The goal is to achieve 30 percent market share but also to help expand the category to $200 million as the new product's features will allow it to compete with more expensive solutions in the larger market. The goal could have a time frame, geographic specificity, and also specific customer segments that are relevant.

The Continuously Iterative Business Plan

Just as in the personal example, the next step is to break this down into the milestones—the 1-year, 2-year, 5-year journey—and understand what the middle game and opening looks like for this product launch. And remember, just as in chess—as you make each move, your options for the next set of moves will shift causing you to rethink, replan, and redirect your resources always with the endgame in mind. Data gathered and analysis techniques refined, your ability to understand a changing set of other factors will cause you to dynamically change your plans.

Often companies will talk about developing a business case or even a business plan and in some cases a full plan is warranted. But be clear about the two ways the process described here is different from the traditional way of thinking about a business plan. The traditional business plan attempts to describe the market (competitors, customers, opportunity, etc.) and the specific actions that will be taken to pursue that market (product development, marketing, sales activities, etc.). Inherent in creating a fixed document is the notion that there is some kind of stasis in the market and an ability to describe actions (and outcomes) in a fixed way. But anyone who has tried to execute on such a plan knows that the real world is much messier, with every aspect of market conditions and competition changing along the way.

So think about developing a kind of continuously iterative business plan into which you build in the expectation that everything will change. Expect market conditions to change, technology to change, and competitors' plans to change—requiring continuous collection and analysis of these shifting conditions that impact your plan. Understand how different kinds of change will cause you to shift tactics—and also recognize that your own actions are opportunities to experiment and learn and provide data that will ultimately change your plans.

The more you think of everything you do as being an iterative series of experiments, the better you will become at collecting the information you need to analyze a situation well. Whenever there is an option to have data gathered, make your request as specific and as complete as possible. Build both the foundation of rich data and the discipline of analysis both for yourself and for your organization and insist that decisions are made both from data and in order to create more data.

All of this talk about data does not eliminate your own ability to observe, use common sense, and use your intuition. But it should help you question instincts that may not make sense in the changing world of the social mobile cloud. Your goal should be to practice analytics combined with intuition as you undergo the process of researching and learning new things in order to move toward achieving the goals in your plans. Here is one example: an airplane pilot has a cockpit of instruments that enable him to fly a plane. The instruments are the analytical tools, with many embedded automated decision-making components. Yet, no pilot would fly without looking out the window, because there are threats that no instrument can predict.

That is a classic example of combining the science of analysis with the art of sound reasoning. As you proceed with figuring out the steps to take to achieve your short- and long-term goals, remember that sound reasoning comes from experience, conservative judgment, and the intuition to ask questions and to push back on assumptions that don't make any sense. If something doesn't make sense to you, don't let your self-doubt and fear make you think that it is your short-coming; that it does make sense but you simply don't understand. The likelihood is that it doesn't make sense. Go through the fact-finding process of analysis to test whether something makes sense, of course, but keep a healthy skepticism, which is your intuition.

On the other end of the reasoning spectrum, when something does make sense but is challenging, your reasoning can help you creatively solve problems. You wouldn't even have goals if it weren't for your ability to see creatively and imagine scenarios. Tap into and trust your intuition as you develop disciplines around data collection and analytics. It will help you select the right data to gather, weed out false information, and recognize a helpful tool, a reliable expert, and an opportunity when you see one.

17

Seven Steps to Adaptability

In the course of this book, I have tried to explain a set of technologies in the social mobile cloud that are fundamentally changing the way our businesses work, our society functions, and even how we behave as individuals. I have offered a set of new business models for you to consider as you think about how these technologies will impact your industry and your life. And I have offered some ideas to help in understanding how change happens, what you can do to get the big picture, and how you can be more effective in making the decisions that are needed to move your business and yourself forward productively.

All of this comes together around the challenge of adaptability—how you respond to change, taking a challenging situation, and learning to not just cope but even thrive in the new environment. These seven steps can help you (and allow you to help your colleagues and your organization) to achieve this adaptability.

Step 1: Why We Resist Change

Understanding why we behave the way we do is essential before we can change our behavior. In understanding our resistance to change, the most important aspect is not to judge yourself. We all are in the same boat—we are hardwired to develop experience, which naturally limits our ability to react to a changed environment. But this is surmountable—we just need to train ourselves to recognize when our experience has become debilitating, and be open to alternatives—especially alternative ways of understanding our circumstances and options.

Step 2: Embrace Data and Analytics

Our businesses and our personal lives now come equipped with rich data gathering tools and analytical models. Develop new, data-rich, and technologically enhanced senses that transform the way you interpret the world. This step enables us to expand our capacity for change. Technology has added new sensory input, and we need to develop our ability to process these signals and use them in our thinking. Imagine functioning in the world not being aware of what your sense of smell is telling you, such as this food is rotten, don't eat it. Once you understand how to use all of the new data you are capable of gathering, it will be like having a new set of senses. And these new senses will enable your ability to change.

Step 3: Understand the Power of Social Collaboration

Our knowledge is being changed by access to collective knowledge, thereby creating new shared knowledge—both in organizations and as individuals in society. This is a pivotal step, because it is where we really understand that we not only have the capacity to change, but that we can accelerate its impact through connecting with family, friends, and colleagues using the social mobile cloud. Key to succeeding in this step is to develop sociological understanding: how we form and draw from collective knowledge, collective consciousness. In this new realm of collaboration, specifically in our ability to offload information from our brains and simply have it available from continuously accessible tools, you can more easily become a systems thinker and see the big picture—essential to your ability to adapt to change.

Step 4: Why We Resist Learning

Distinct from step 1, resisting change, we also resist learning new things. The reasons run the gamut from fear of failure, to believing we're too good for it. Here we take the concepts from step 1 and apply them to understanding that our traditional institutional learning system, borne from Industrial Age thinking, is detrimental to personal and societal change because it is based on negative reinforcement and the notion that there are right and wrong answers and that there are consequences for being wrong. But once you recognize the need for constant learning and accept that being wrong is part of the learning process, you'll be ready to develop new skills and gain new knowledge.

Step 5: Use New Learning Tools

Learning doesn't have to happen in a classroom. Along with the idea of constant learning comes a range of new technological tools and systems of learning. Online movies are the new lecture halls—literally as institutions like MIT and Stanford have demonstrated by putting their coursework online. Communities and discussion forums create the classroom space where we can interact with one another—explaining concepts, debating interpretations, and developing new ideas. Educational institutions had largely remained unchanged since medieval colleges—convenient ways to aggregate instructors and students. But the social mobile cloud has deconstructed learning and now allows you to learn wherever, whenever, whatever, and at your own pace.

Step 6: Learn to Use Systems Thinking

In short, systems thinking is learning how to see the big picture and have access to details when necessary, but not expend your energy on minutiae so you don't suffer from information overload. Systems thinking is efficient, clarifying, and empowering. With systems thinking, you can maneuver and negotiate any circumstance in the modern world. Achieving this step is a critical step because it leads to better decision making and the ability to understand how to overcome your experience and intuition when aspects of your environment have changed.

Step 7: Decision Making

It is surprising that we are never formally taught good decision-making skills—not in school and not in the workplace. Yet, it is the most important thing we do, in every facet of everyday life. As discussed in Chapter 16, a new approach to decision making, based on data and analytics, is the final step in adaptability. By approaching change rigorously, collecting data, and developing our analytical capabilities we can make good decisions even when our intuition is telling us to do something else.

Afterword

Digital Transformation: What Will You and Your Business
Look Like 10, 20, 50 Years from Now?

Over the course of human civilization, we have seen the steady reduction in the number of people working in agriculture. Advances in technology have done two things: increased the productive capacity of the land (irrigation, fertilizer, engineered seeds) and increased the productivity of each individual worker (plow, tractor, cultivator). With each new generation of technology, the output per acre and per individual has increased, allowing us to feed an ever-growing population with the labor of a diminishing percentage of that population.

During the past 200 years, the Industrial Revolution has also been having the same impact on other categories of labor. The introduction of process and mechanization has made it easier to produce more and more goods with fewer and fewer people. What is the end state? Are we heading toward a zero labor world?

This is a moment of complete change in state of being: an ice cube transformed into liquid, a rigid structure now dynamic fluid. This is what we are heading toward—everything we have done over thousands of years to develop the most effective means of organizing and managing our collective productive energies could be obsolete in the next few decades.

When your objective is to marshal a group's physical output, it is essential to do two things very clearly: define specific roles and actions for each person, and structure a hierarchy in which individuals are supervised and directed to fill those roles and perform those actions. Ancient Sparta's success as a military power came from following these two rules. Each soldier knew his role next to his fellow soldier and each group had their leader. If your unit pivoted to the left, you went to the left. The individual had very little discretion. Similarly in the Industrial Revolution we learned to specialize our labor and work harmoniously with one another by exercising little individual discretion.

Undoing the discipline of thousands of years will be difficult but we must do so if we are to achieve the next level of human evolution. Our brains and not our brawn will dominate work in the future. So we don't need to marshal physical output. Physical output will be the work of machines.

For us to think effectively, we will need to communicate differently with one another. The muscles of our bodies can no longer be trained to all move to the left when we are told as a group to do so. Instead, the power of each intellect will need to contribute to the collective outcome. Our brains, unlike our muscles, add the most value when we stand out and offer differentiated value to the whole, not pull together.

To stand out we need one another in a new way. We need to collaborate in a truly effective manner, one that finds balance: first the individual ideas, then the sum that is greater than the parts. The fractalized workplace is thankfully creating the autonomy for individual intellects to be heard again, instead of the legacy of the Industrial Age: the stifling, mob-mentality cube workplace.

Social mobile cloud technology is of course what is enabling fractalization and the sheer rapidity of change. And therein lies our answer: how we will undo the discipline of thousands of years and re-create businesses, industries, and economies so that the best ideas can flourish.

Changes will be mediated by technology, and our individual success will depend on our ability to adapt to and embrace these technologies. The specifics of the changes and the technologies are hard to predict. But these general outlines can tell us something about how to live in this new world and what choices to make. The world of 10, 20, and 50 years from now will be substantially more different from today than the world of 10, 20, and 50 years ago was by comparison. As the rate of change increases, we can expect the differences to continue to be greater, even while the time spans are comparable.

We have learned from the predictions of the past that the future is unlikely to resemble our imaginations, since those visions are dependent on what we know today. Just as it would have been very difficult for someone in the 1960s to predict the implications of the microcomputer, we find it impossible to know how technology in the labs today will transform our world in the coming decades.

The one predictable outcome is change itself, so ultimately we must prepare ourselves for adaptability. Some glimpses into the future that we might have to adapt to:

10–15 Years from Now

The trends that will define the world in the next decade are already in place and while we can't know how a big breakthrough might change our world there are two big state changes we can predict. We already know that computers will continue to become smaller, communications more pervasive, and our use of them more embedded in everything we do which will thoroughly change the way we interact with the world and with one another. And on a macro scale, private enterprise is already successfully launching rockets into earth orbit, and plans exist for commercial space exploration on the moon and beyond.

One possibility—computation may transform perception. Our eyes and ears could have a computational mediation. When we look at something, augmented or annotated reality would overlay information. As I mentioned earlier in this book, our children will likely grow up with a very different idea about what reality is—they will expect the physical world and data that overlays and transforms what we can immediately know about that world. Some of the problems that we have today, such as navigating a country where we don't know the language, will no longer even be noticed as problems. The signs and speaker's voices will be instantly translated into a language we understand.

At the same time that we are expanding our local reality through information and communication, we will also be expanding from a global to a solar system–wide civilization. Space travel may finally be a commercial reality, not just something governments can afford to do. In a decade, we would likely still be a long way from vacations on the moon, but there are real projects under way to put a commercial space station "hotel" into orbit. And satellite exploration, mining on the moon, and plans for travel even farther into our solar system will be unfolding. This isn't science fiction—it is starting to happen today.

15–30 Years from Now

Computing will of course continue to evolve, but we should also see the beginnings of some important changes in the infrastructure we use to support life on our planet. The growing demand for energy to support all of the technology we use, an increasing population (that is also increasingly wealthy), which will want more of this technology (to say nothing of more food and more shelter), and one possibility is that a growing number of robots could change the way we produce energy, food, and fresh water.

Computing will further change how we interact with the world. Our ability to recall past events could be altered by easily accessible ubiquitous recordings of everything around us. Have trouble remembering where you left the car or what your spouse asked you to get at the grocery store? You might simply replay the moment when you parked or were given the list.

Every surface, from kitchen counters to street signs, may someday be capable of being information rich and interactive. Computing has the potential to be embedded so deeply into the things we use that we won't see it any more as a computer. It could just seem like a refrigerator—but one that knows what is in it and can place an order to replace items. Or the toaster that can detect when the bread is burning and turn itself off, or the car that knows when it needs servicing and can place its own request for an appointment.

But perhaps the most important challenge facing humanity is having a reliable and clean energy source. Saving energy is not a long-term solution to the planet's problems. Instead, we need to use more energy. We need abundant energy that we can use to create more clean water, more healthy food, more products that we use, and places to live. Could solar energy supply a greater proportion of our needs within the next 20 years? The pace at which solar cells are being manufactured, and the rate at which they are improving suggests the same doubling effect that we have seen in computer technology. Combined with innovation in other energy areas, we can expect massive changes in the next 20 years.

New energy sources will allow more people to have and consume more goods with a reduced impact on the planet. This will be essential to political and social stability as it will move more people into the educated portion of the population, capable of earning a livelihood through their brains instead of through labor.

50 Years from Now

Think about the world of 50 years ago—the early 1960s—and compare the lives and work of people then to ours today. Now try to imagine a world different from todays by that same degree. Then double or triple the amount of change. You might still fall short. It is very difficult to imagine how our great grandchildren will live—but many of us will be around to see. Healthcare improvements have continued to stack up and might continue to do so—adding additional high quality years to lives that have already seen enormous expansion of longevity over the past century. If the rate of improvement in life span per year of medical research continues, we could easily see *average* life spans at well over 100.

By then, we may be mining the moon and perhaps elsewhere in the solar system. We might have fully extended the sense in which we are linked to computer and communication networks at all times. Robots and automated manufacturing could have replaced almost all of the physical labor needed to produce goods or even perform most services.

I close with these thoughts because I hope you will understand that the social mobile cloud that this book began with is only one step in a longer journey. Even as we adapt to these new technologies, the world is continuing to change and new demands on our adaptability are emerging. What will you and your business need to do to stay relevant in 10, 20, or 50 years? We will need to continue to ADAPT in order to be around and part of this exciting future.

A P P E N D I X

PwC Thought Leadership on Social, Mobile, Analytics, Cloud (SMAC)

Section 1: Social

(i) Consumer Activity on Social Media Sites Dwarfs that of Health-Care Companies, Finds New PwC Study on Social Media in Health Care

April 17, 2012
   http://bit.ly/PwC_ConsumerActivityonSocialMediaSites

Abstract. Social media is changing the nature of health-care inter-action, and health organizations that ignore this virtual environment may be missing opportunities to engage consumers, according to a new report by the Health Research Institute (HRI) at PwC US titled, "Social Media Likes Healthcare: From Marketing to Social Business." The report found that social media activity by hospitals, health insurers, and pharmaceutical companies is miniscule compared with the activity on community sites. While 8 in 10 health-care companies (as tracked by HRI during a sample one-week period) had a presence on various social media sites, community sites had 24 times more social media activity than corporate sites. The finding holds significant implications for businesses seeking to capitalize on social media opportunities.

Excerpt. "The power of social media for health organizations is in listening and engaging with consumers on their terms. Social media has created a new customer service access point where consumers expect an immediate response." —Kelly Barnes, U.S. health industries leader, PwC

(ii) Social Media "Likes" Healthcare: From Marketing to Social Business

April 2012
   http://bit.ly/PwC_Social17_April2012

Abstract.   This report dives into the social world of the health industry and provides insights into new and emerging relationships between consumers and the biggest health companies that serve them. It examines how individuals think about and use the social channel; how some providers, insurers, medical device and pharmaceutical companies are responding; discusses specific implications for organizations to take advantage of this new view into the twenty-first-century patient.

Outline.

- Executive summary
- Social media is changing online dialogue from one-to-many to many-to-many, at a phenomenal speed
- Consumers are broadcasting their wants, needs, and preferences through social media
  - Social animals
  - Social studies
  - Social skills
  - Social speed
  - Social networks
  - Social currency
- How health organizations are evolving from social media marketing to social business strategy
- A future look: Data generated from individuals can help complete the patient profile
- What this means for your business

Excerpt.   Business strategies that include social media can help health industry companies to take a more active, engaged role in managing individuals' health. Social marketing can evolve into social business with the right leadership and investment of resources.

Organizations should coordinate internally to effectively integrate information from the social media space and connect with their customers in more meaningful ways that provide value and increase trust. Insights from social media also offer instant feedback on products or services, along with new ideas for innovation. Organizations that can incorporate this information into their operations will be better positioned to meet the needs of today's consumers.

(iii) SEC Staff Provides Guidance on the Use of Social Media by Advisers

2012
http://bit.ly/PwC_Social13_2012

Abstract. While many investment advisers have adopted written policies and procedures addressing social media use, this risk alert sets forth a number of specific factors that the Securities and Exchange Commission (SEC) staff believes should be considered if and when an adviser and its personnel are permitted to use social media.

Outline.

- What is social media?
- Compliance program considerations
- Third-party content
- Record keeping
- Points to consider

Excerpt. Reflecting the fact that many registered investment advisers and their personnel use social media in various forms to communicate with existing and potential clients and to promote their services, the SEC staff recently issued a National Examination Risk Alert providing suggestions for complying with the antifraud, compliance, and recordkeeping provisions of the federal securities laws.

This is the first time that the SEC staff has provided guidance concerning the use of social media by advisers.

(iv) Podcast: The Real Value of Social Media

January 17, 2012
http://bit.ly/PwC_RealValueOfSocialMedia

Abstract.   This podcast touches on the following:

- Are the right people engaged and trained on how to deal with social media and do you have the right technology in place to evolve?
- Integrate your channels—make sure you have the right communication lines inside to support your customer.
- Have a voice and presence in social media.
- Develop the ability to co-create with your customers and employees—developing new products or a forum to deal with issues.

(v) Social Media: The New Business Reality for Board Directors

2012
   http://bit.ly/PwC_Social14_2012

Abstract.   In social channels, customers create their own version of company ads on YouTube, whistleblowers use blogs and social communities to spread news like wildfire, employees can respond to internal requests for expertise in a nanosecond, and small firms have the reach of global brands by engaging communities anywhere in the world. This article explores how social media can help you protect and improve shareholder value.

Excerpt.   Social networks, media sharing sites, microblogs, online games, and product review sites are all part of everyday life. Current media darlings like Facebook, Twitter, and YouTube were unknown brands a few years ago, but now these social platforms have massive appeal and people from all age groups and demographics are signing up to take part. The global adoption of this phenomenon has a direct impact on your organization as employees, customers, investors, and stakeholders participate in social communities. Don't underestimate the new rules of engagement.

(vi) Joining the Conversation: Life Sciences Industry Ventures into Social Media Despite Regulatory Uncertainty

2011
   http://bit.ly/PwC_Social18_2011

Abstract.   Social media dialogue, often driven by bloggers and other key influencers, holds the potential for more relevant customer feedback and market insight than any previous communications channel. For the life sciences industry, social media also opens new opportunities to collaborate with scientific and health-care provider communities on research and product development.

Outline.

- Social media explosion presents multiple opportunities for customer interaction and market insight
- Address strategy, organization, process, technology, sustainability—and inherent risks
- Take the next step

Excerpt.   A PricewaterhouseCoopers survey of 3,500 consumers in seven countries found that more people go to the Internet (48 percent) to find information to make decisions about their healthcare than to doctors (43 percent). Health-related social media sites, such as PatientsLikeMe, which enables people to share information with others who face similar health challenges, are gaining in popularity.

(vii) Connecting with Social Media

2011
    http://bit.ly/PwC_Social16_2011

Abstract.   This article offers advice on how to get started with social media for private companies.

Outline.

- Explore
- Start listening
- Develop a plan
- Choose the optimal social media platform to achieve your goals
- Create your presence and establish your voice
- Manage the conversation
- Coordinate channels
- Think mobile
- Stay connected

Excerpt.   The power and influence of social media is being felt just about everywhere these days—from the political and social spheres to the businesses and personal ones. For private companies, the opportunities social media offers are as far-ranging as the options to connect. It can play a leading role in helping to drive business by engaging employees, consumers, suppliers, partners, and even investors and turning them into champions of your company's brand or extensions of your customer service departments. Even better, the cost of entry is low. More often than not, it's just a matter of the time and effort you are willing to put into it.

(viii) Engage Customers through Social Media

2011
   http://bit.ly/PwC_Social15_2011

Abstract.   In the rest of this article we explain what social media is and how it differs from, and is similar to, traditional marketing and communication media. We look at some of the reasons the leaders are successful and what lessons they may offer. We also explore the potential value of social media for business and most important how to get started and successfully grow in this dynamic, burgeoning marketplace.

Outline.

- How big is social media?
  - It's bigger than you think
  - Popular platforms
- What are the leaders doing?
  - Social media and financial services
- What makes social media different?
  - Case study
- Why should you care?
- What are the implications for your business?
  - How to balance security and social networking
- How can you get started?
  - Tools you can use to start listening

Excerpt.   "It takes years, not weeks, to embed consumer conversations in an organization. Companies need to address this now or it will be a huge challenge to catch up." —Anthony van der Hoek, Director of Strategy and Business Solutions at Coca-Cola

(ix) The Power of Social Media

2011
  http://bit.ly/PwC_Social12_2011

Abstract. This article emphasizes that social media can create a collaborative dialogue with a very large but very specific audience—one person at a time. It breaks down formal barriers. While it should not replace face-to-face communication, it can enhance the overall customer experience and create new sales and servicing opportunities.

Outline.

  - What are the challenges and implications for CIOs?
  - What are the benefits?
  - What are the risks?
  - What is the evolution of social media?
  - Social media success stories
  - How can we help you build value?

Excerpt. "Social media has been described as a channel, a platform—and even an online conversation. Unfortunately, none of these descriptors do any justice to CIOs when trying to get the buy-in of their colleagues. At PwC, we see social media for what it is—a business tool that can be used to solve real business issues." —Debbie Dimoff, PwC Technology Consulting

(x) Social Media Opens New Interaction Channel for Medtech Companies and Their Customers, Enhancing Innovation Opportunities

December 2011
  http://bit.ly/PwC_ThoughtLeadershipRegistration

Abstract. Companies that rely on innovation cannot afford to omit social media for sales and marketing, product development, and business relationships from their business strategy. This brief addresses the impact of the popularity of social media, regulatory challenges that remain, the ability to engage and learn from patients and professionals, as well as how to develop a compliant yet results-driven, enterprise-level social media program.

Outline.

- Regulatory challenges slow industry's adoption of social media
- Potential to engage and learn from patients and professionals beckons
- Effective use requires a well-planned, systematic approach
- Building a community of innovation

Excerpt.   Although the medical technology industry has been slower to adopt social media than those that are less regulated, a few pioneers have emerged on Facebook, Twitter, and YouTube. Their efforts have mostly focused on "safe" uses of social media, such as education about the use of their products and disease awareness. For example, the International Diabetes Foundation has recognized Boston Scientific's social media efforts to raise awareness of diabetes and the World Diabetes Day campaign.

(xi) The Consumerization of IT: The Next-Generation CIO

November 2011
    http://bit.ly/PwC_Social7_November2011

Abstract.   This paper explains the fundamental drivers of information technology (IT) consumerization and shows how the chief information officer (CIO) can embrace that force for the good of both the enterprise and the user.

Outline.

- An expression of a deeper shift in workplace expectations
- The consumerization of IT is really about societal change
- The CIO challenge: Forging an adult relationship with users
- How CIOs benefit from the consumerization of IT
- A new IT architecture for a new business relationship
- A framework for a CIO in the era of consumerized IT
- Consumerization isn't about technology management
- CIOs must embrace a democratic management approach

Excerpt. The "consumerization of IT"—defined as the use of technologies that can easily be provisioned by non-technologists—is currently a hot topic among CIOs. Today's consumerization of IT trends is the culmination of a fundamental shift in the relationship between employers and employees—especially professionals—that began four decades ago. This shift has only now worked its way into the world of enterprise technology. To be successful, CIOs need to be more proactive. In accepting the inevitability of the consumerization trend and preparing for it by rethinking how they run IT, CIOs should consider forging new, collaborative relationships with users, giving them freedom to make IT decisions, and teaching them how to assume responsibility for those decisions. And rather than enforcing hardware and application standards, they will need to rethink IT architecture and controls to focus on controlling—or loosening controls on—information.

(xii) Podcast: Lessons Learned from the Economist Online

November 2, 2011
    http://bit.ly/PwC_Social20_November2011

Abstract. In this episode of *Strategy Talks*, guests Andrew Light and Nick Blunden, global managing director and publisher of *The Economist* online, discuss the rapid changes to content in the digital space and what businesses need to do in order to keep pace.

(xiii) PwC Survey Shows B2B Companies Are Running Blind into the Social Media World

September 29, 2011
    http://bit.ly/PwC_Social27_September2011

Abstract. PwC's new paper "Uncovering B2B Social Media: Value, Innovation, and Engagement" surveyed the attitudes of companies to social media to show the levels of "social media maturity." The survey revealed that although B2B companies are investing financially in social media, they are not backing this up with clear strategies to their staff on the use of social media or by investing in the people resources necessary to make it work effectively—less than 12 percent of organizations surveyed have full-time social media teams in place.

(xiv) Podcast—Social Media: Why Your Business Can't Afford to Ignore It

September 9, 2011
   http://bit.ly/PwC_Social19_September2011

Abstract.   We have all heard the popular saying "The medium is the message." Never was this more true than in the case of social media. This podcast is an interview with PwC's Debbie Dimoff, who discusses why social media tools and practices are becoming increasingly crucial for business interactions with customers, and for monitoring the wider business landscape around you.

(xv) Technology Forecast: Transforming Collaboration with Social Tools

Issue 3, 2011
   http://bit.ly/PwC_Social1_2011Issue3

Abstract.   This issue of *Technology Forecast* explores how to confront communications overload and boost collaboration potential by making the best use of the new powerful social tools. Business is inherently social, which is why collaboration and communications that scale are so fundamental. So why aren't enterprises making more effective use of social networking tools internally? It is because most employees are already overwhelmed by distracting, irrelevant, and numerous requests to communicate.

Outline.

- **The collaboration paradox: More social information helps the workforce find what they're looking for.** First, we had communication silos inside organizations. Now with e-mail and the Web, we're all dealing with communications chaos. Paradoxically, the metadata—the context around the communications that new social technologies are now surfacing—offers the secret to eliminating communications chaos, moving enterprises closer to fully shared knowledge. Analytics that take advantage of this metadata are the first step.
- **Enterprise success with emerging social technology: Innovators are learning to build graphs to help users find the information they need—and one another.** One thing enterprises have learned is that siloed, standalone consumer Web-style

microblogging or social networking tools rarely work well inside an enterprise. Social technology that is embedded in the enterprise application environment to offer collaborative support to specific business processes, or explicitly targeted at unifying all communications and collaboration, can be much more useful.

- **The CIO's role in social enterprise strategy: An evolutionary approach.** Before trying to add to the mix, take stock of how your workforce is collaborating to begin with. What is the appropriate rationale for adopting a new tool in this case? By formulating an adoption process with goal setting and incentives appropriate to the business, CIOs can help business units position themselves for the collaboration and filtering potential of emerging social networking platforms.

Excerpt. At first glance, you might think that social networks just add to the problem. Most companies today are adopting social networking internally without a good plan for taking advantage of its latent potential. They aren't understanding that each employee's enterprise social network is the best way to filter and manage electronic communications so that employees attend to them in their order of importance and potential value. In fact, the social analytics available from the leading enterprise social tools are the first addition to the toolset for electronic communications that can actually reduce the overhead of dealing with enterprise communications.

(xvi) Enterprise Success with Emerging Social Technology

August 2011
    http://bit.ly/PwC_Social9_August2011

Abstract. In conversations with some of the most fully engaged adopters of social technology, CIOs, and social technology leaders, PwC sees a change occurring in the enterprise social technology landscape and the opportunity for organizations to take advantage of it. Enterprise social technology has moved from a divergent phase into a more convergent phase. Understanding this evolution and where the advantage lies will be crucial to mapping a strategy to improve online collaboration. This article describes how social technology has evolved and evaluates how it will impact the enterprise in the next five years. This article is not intended to be a comprehensive vendor review; rather, this article assesses how the technology itself has evolved, and it uses examples from several vendors.

Outline.

- Standalone social solutions: Generation one
- Integrated social technology: Generation two
- Integrating social functionality into everyday work
- Managing the new enterprise social content
- The future states of social technology: Generation three
- The rise of the enterprise interest graph
- How social graphs relate to interest graphs
- Dynamic search and triple store support the social graph

Excerpt.   Enterprise social technologies have evolved through two generations, and a third one is now emerging. The first generation (late 1990s to early 2000s) primarily comprised standalone solutions that had narrowly focused functionality. The second generation (mid-2000s to 2010) comprised broader tools that included some better integration, curation, and analysis capabilities. Emerging enterprise social technology is now in a third generation (beginning 2011), which will evolve to provide much richer semantic understanding of data—more sophisticated social graphing that adds to the infra-structure-oriented architecture that allows organizations to embed the tools in existing application suites.

(xvii) The New Digital Tipping Point

2011
    http://bit.ly/PwC_Social29_2011

Abstract.   There is increasing regulation and continuing cost pressures for banks. This is being compounded by the persistent trend in margin compression and alarming market uncertainty. The emergence of new technologies into banking has had a permanent impact, as once traditional banking revenue pools are now being sucked up by new competitors, especially in the payments' space. All of this is happening at a time when customer expectations for banking services (both offline and online) are being reset by the experiences being provided by retailers and online providers, elsewhere. Finally, to this long list add the general lack of trust customers have in financial services—owing to the credit crunch—and the general perception that the major banks all contributed to the global market collapse. We can quickly conclude that traditional banking is facing its steepest challenge in more than a generation.

This article argues that a new tipping point has been reached with digital at its fulcrum, and it explains why this is so.

Outline.

- Introduction: Driving customer value through digital
- Customer relationship primacy is the new source of value in banking
- Digital is crucial in addressing changing customer behaviour
- Customers value new digital offerings
- New digital entrants are disrupting the banking ecosystem
- The battle for customer relationship primacy among banks has begun

Excerpt.   The growth of mobile has significant implications for banks. As mobile phones get equipped with more and better functionality, it will transform the traditional interaction model with the consumer. Well-appointed branches and slick websites will no longer be enough, as customers expect services on the move. Location-based offers, timely and relevant content, and interactive applications will form the basis of the mobile customer's engagement with their banks.

(xviii) The Wisdom of Crowds

October 2010
   http://bit.ly/PwC_Social10_October2010

Abstract.   Retail and consumer brands are more closely followed by social media users than any other type of brand. Those retailers and consumer packaged goods (CPG) companies that understand how to harness the power of social media can directly affect the perception of their organizations, connect directly with customers to gain their insights, and react quickly in times of reputational crisis.

Outline.

- The wisdom of crowds
- A little consumer conversation can make a good marketing campaign even better
- Customers—your partners in innovation
- Employees—your brand ambassadors
- Playing digital defense

Excerpt. "There are two ways of doing it. You could wait for something to go wrong and then use the community to fix it, but why not leverage the creative ability in the community that's already out there?"—David Cousino, Unilever Consumer Marketing Insights Global Category Director

(xix) Social Media Is Fueling the Reinvention of the Customer Experience

Fall 2010
   http://bit.ly/PwC_Social22_Fall2010

Abstract. This article suggests that social media can be a powerful way of providing financial information to customers of the products and services they use, as they need it. Providing customers with "on-demand" information, easily accessible through various social media channels, can reap rewards in customer acquisition, retention, and loyalty.

Outline.

- The five things you should know about social media
- The value of social media
- How to take advantage of social media to improve the customer experience

Excerpt. There are a number of ways to use social media for positive results. So what exactly are the value drivers of social media? Let's keep it really simple. Wouldn't you like to gain positive brand reputation, make money, and save costs? In the olden days of the Internet and banking, it was tempting to fall into believing the nouveau return on investment (ROI) of the times like sticky websites and increase in eyeballs. We had loads of fun, vivid phrases, but they didn't equate to real business returns.

(xx) PwC's View on the Maturing of Social Networking into a Business Discipline

February 2010
    http://bit.ly/PwC_Social25_February2010

Abstract.   PwC believes that the time has come for organizations to develop a logical framework for using social networking by integrating the techniques with the organization's business objectives. The real challenge is how to integrate social collaboration with the well-established collection of operational models now in use in industry, entertainment and media, banking, and commerce. Social collaboration over time needs to become a complementary, integrated channel.

Outline.

- PwC views on the maturing of social networking into a business discipline
- Human behavior: participative, critical, and demanding
- How consumer conversation will transform business

Excerpt.   The real challenge is how to integrate social collaboration with the well-established collection of operational models now in use in industry, entertainment and media, banking, and commerce. Social collaboration over time needs to become a complementary, integrated channel

(xxi) Security for Social Networking

2010
    http://bit.ly/PwC_Social11_2010

Abstract.   This article introduces the ways in which social media can enrich employee performance, as well as some of the serious risks to an enterprise's network, data, and reputation. Ultimately it examines business implications.

Outline.

- The heart of the matter
- An in-depth discussion
- What this means for your business

Excerpt.   The strategy must be two-pronged: It must set forth policies and procedures that govern the use of social networks and corporate information, and it must use technology that helps protect the safety and integrity of data and the corporate network. This multilayered approach requires that the business and technology sides of the company unite and fully commit to the initiative. The two must analyze content and policies in detail, as well as determine the right mix of enterprise technologies available to monitor, classify, and manage data.

(xxii) Transformers

Winter 2009
    http://bit.ly/PwC_Social3_Winter2009

Abstract.   Today's pace of change is relentless. In this article from our business magazine *View*, discover how technology innovations like cloud computing, virtualization, enterprise Web 2.0, and business performance platforms are helping companies become more agile to better manage change.

Outline.

- Today's relentless pace of change
- New way forward, new approaches
- Reducing complexity: Toward a cleaner slate
- Virtualization
- Cloud computing
- Application rationalization and portfolio management
- Master data management
- Web 2.0: Power to the people
- Business intelligence: Smarter and faster decision making
- Investing for the future
- Tech forecast
- Looking back to look forward

- Tools for managing change
- Ten technologies that build agile businesses

Excerpt.   In our work with clients, we have observed that the nature of organizational change itself has changed. It has gone from episodic—that is, one major upheaval at a time—to a continuous stream of competing, overlapping, and accelerating shifts, all of which must be dealt with at the same time. Gone is the luxury of focusing on a single key initiative like a billion-dollar corporate acquisition. More often, a business must also focus on other make-or-break projects simultaneously, such as waging a multimillion-dollar patent infringement case or securing a promising joint venture in China. Add to that the shock waves resulting from the current economic situation, and the environment becomes even more dynamic.

(xxiii) PwC View: Issue 5

January 2007
    http://bit.ly/PwC_Social23_January2007

Abstract.   New Web technologies have turned consumers into innovators: communicating, networking and collaborating with each other in ways unthinkable just five years ago. Tom Coates, who specializes in social media at Yahoo!, uses the term *structured mediation* to describe how the Web's content and social networking tools—often called Web 2.0 technologies—have made consumer created content increasingly relevant and useful, enabling infinite possibilities for building communities and creating value. This new breed of socially networked consumer is driving corporate innovation, creating new business models, and changing established ones.

Outline.

- Social networks
- Consumers making connections
- Employees making connections
- Enhancing employee networks
- Information security
- Bridging the divide between physical and digital information security

- Privacy under pressure and the changing face of identity verification
- Becoming a prepared acquirer
- Finding the good, avoiding the bad
- Postmerger integration planning evident in convergence-driven deals
- U.S entertainment and media outlook
- Fresh eyes

(xxiv) The Rise of Lifestyle Media: Achieving Success in the Digital Convergence Era

2006
　http://bit.ly/PwC_Social4_2006

Abstract. The consumer media landscape is radically changing: Content and services are overflowing while consumer time and attention remains limited. A new approach that helps consumers maximize their limited time and attention to create a rich, personalized, and social media environment is needed. PwC calls this approach *lifestyle media*; it is the combination of a personalized media experience with a social context for participation.

Excerpt. Consumers are increasingly calling the shots in a converged media world. They use Apple iPods to make their own music playlists. Personal video recorders allow them to customize television lineups. Satellite radios pump commercial-free music into their cars. These consumers pull stock-market updates, text messages, and download wallpaper, ringtones, and short-form video into their mobile phones. They come together in online communities, generate their own content, mix it, and share it on a growing number of social networks. No longer a captive, mass media audience, today's media consumer is unique, demanding, and engaged.

Section 2: Mobile

(i) Device Connectivity Speed: One Half of an Equation

October 2012
　http://bit.ly/PwC_Mobile16_2012

Abstract.　From the user's perspective, the mobile experience starts with the speed at which the device receives data and applications.

That speed is the combined result of the speed capability of the modem technology inside the device, which is fixed, and the speed capability of the infrastructure, which can vary. Thus, wireless speed is a complicated component to measure. So complicated, in fact, that the Mobile Technologies Index breaks it into two components, each with its own metric:

- Device connectivity speed (in megabits per second per dollar [Mbps/$])
- Infrastructure speed in average megabits per second (Mbps)

This article provides our forecast for device connectivity speed, explaining the metric and how we calculate it, and explores some implications for mobile innovation.

PwC forecasts a compound annual growth rate of 37 percent for average aggregated device connectivity speed as measured in Mbps/ $ through 2015. Put another way, average aggregated device connectivity speed will be four times greater in 2015 than in 2011.

Outline.

- Making sense of the rapid change in mobile innovation
- Device connectivity speed: One half of an equation
- Infrastructure speed: Watch capital investment in 4G for the next inflection
- Application processors: Driving the next wave of innovation

Excerpt. "Mobile is one of several disruptive changes affecting technology, communications, and media industries. The others being cloud computing, social media, and the network of intelligent devices through the Internet." "The individual impact of each could threaten established vendors and create new customer value propositions— something mobile is already demonstrating in spades. But their combined impact is likely to be greater as mobile devices engage with smart objects without user intervention, incorporate personal data stored in the cloud, and socialize commerce. We expect the same level of disruption we have seen in the mobile ecosystem to play out in all corners of the technology industry, in some cases bringing former competitors together and in others turning friends into rivals."
—Vicki Huff, Technology Industry Partner in Silicon Valley

(ii) Intelligent Health Care through mHealth

September 30, 2012
http://bit.ly/PwC_Mobile30_2012

Abstract. New mobile information technologies, combined with innovative business models, offer consumers the promise of greater control over their health, more choices, better access, and a decrease in overall costs. We call this new paradigm intelligent health care, and it is primed for significant global growth, with benefits such as:

- Apps that act as a "clinician in a box"—using sensors, algorithms, and artificial intelligence designed to simulate the advice of a clinician
- Empowering patients to self-help and learn healthier behaviors, while helping transform health care into a more productive state
- Tools offering constant expert clinical advice and support, particularly for chronic diseases that require continual management

PwC can help developers of "intelligent" health-care apps navigate the regulatory requirements, ensure clinical efficacy, determine payment structures—and leverage the abundant opportunities available in this area of growing market interest.

Excerpt. Patient engagement is not the only driver for more intelligent health care. As we look forward to the challenges of all health-care systems, we find that all require a dramatic increase in productivity. In 1980, we had on average 10 patients for every health-care worker and only spent about 8 percent of our GDP on health care and had virtually no shortages of doctors or nurses (see the full article for more information). In 2020, however, the landscape looks quite different. By then the United States will be spending over 20 percent of GDP on health care, will have an 800,000-person shortfall in doctors and nurses, and will accommodate three patients per health-care provider (see the full article for more information). Such a state is unsustainable. Yet by applying intelligent health-care tools, applications, and devices through mHealth, and empowering patients to self-help, they will get the support necessary to transform health care into a much higher productive state.

(iii) PwC Survey of Global Mobility Policies

August 30, 2012
    http://bit.ly/PwC_Mobile7_August2012

Abstract.   PwC is pleased to announce the availability of our survey. In today's highly competitive global marketplace, the structure and appropriateness of your global mobility policies can have a significant impact on your organization. Examining your global mobility policies will allow you to determine if they are comprehensive, effective, and properly aligned with your organizational goals.

Policy benchmarking remains the primary springboard to achieving a more competitive profile in your market, greater success in managing your mobile population, and, ultimately, better financial results for your organization.

(iv) PwC Introduces Mobile Innovations Forecast, Provides Early Notice of Disruptions and Opportunities in Technology Sector

July 26, 2012
    http://bit.ly/PwC_Mobile23_July2012

Abstract.   The PwC Mobile Technologies Index is the starting point for PwC's ongoing forecasting efforts in mobile innovation. In addition to the Mobile Technologies Index, future PwC MIF articles will explore different aspects of the four-part framework, including new capabilities of emerging and existing technologies; new use cases that arise from performance improvements or entirely new mobile technologies including the extension of the mobile ecosystem into the cloud; and new business models that might increasingly rely on industry dynamics outside of the mobile industry itself. The MIF is part of PwC's framework for understanding the dynamics driving the broader technology, communications and entertainment, and media markets.

(v) Emerging mHealth: Paths for Growth

June 28, 2012
    http://bit.ly/PwC_EmergingmHealth

Abstract.   Mobile technology's role in health care is piquing interest across the globe for its potential to address long-standing issues in health-care provision. This PwC-commissioned report from the Economist Intelligence Unit (EIU) looks at the development of mHealth in 10 countries (5 developed and 5 emerging) and the role that various stakeholders—from health-care payers to physicians and patients—can play in its development. These insights will help us understand its evolution and how it will transform health care as we know it today.

Outline.

- The current landscape
- Expectation versus reality
- Colliding interests, competing visions
- Health-care innovation: A school of patience
- Emerging markets, emerging solutions
- From technology to solutions worth buying

Excerpt.   Health care is moving toward a precision-based model—or "personalized medicine." As a result of greater understanding of the human genome, together with other personalized technologies, the industry will likely transform—as have many other industries—to one that is predictive, personalized, participatory, and preventive. mHealth will be a major factor in providing personal toolkits that will ultimately help those manage predicted vulnerabilities, chronic illness, and episodic acute conditions. Enabled by technology, connectivity, and data, mass customization is on the horizon allowing mHealth solutions to flourish.

(vi) Consumers Are Ready to Adopt Mobile Health Faster than the Health Industry Is Prepared to Adapt, Finds PwC Study on Global mHealth Adoption

June 7, 2012
    http://bit.ly/PwC_Mobile15_June2012

Abstract.   Widespread adoption of mobile technology in health care, or mHealth, is now viewed as inevitable in both developed and emerging markets around the world, but the pace of adoption will likely be led by emerging markets and lag consumer demand, according to a new global study conducted for PwC Global Healthcare by the Economist Intelligence Unit.

The groundbreaking study "Emerging mHealth: Paths for Growth" found that consumers have high expectations for mHealth, particularly in developing economies as mobile cellular subscriptions there become ubiquitous. In emerging markets, consumers perceive mHealth as a way to increase access to health care while patients in developed markets see it as a way to improve the convenience, cost, and quality of health care.

According to PwC, if the promise of mHealth is realized by consumers, the impact on health-care delivery could be significant and fundamentally alter traditional relationships within the health-care industry. The use of mHealth and speed of adoption will be determined in each country by stakeholders' response to mHealth as a disruptive innovation to overcome structural impediments and align interests around patients' needs and expectations.

Excerpt. "Despite demand and the obvious potential benefits of mHealth, rapid adoption is not yet occurring. The main barriers are not the technology but rather systemic to health care and inherent resistance to change. Though many people think mobile health will be ancillary or bolted on to the health-care industry, we look at it differently: mHealth is the future of health care, deeply integrated into delivery that will be better, faster, less expensive, and far more customer-focused." —David Levy, MD, Global Healthcare Leader, PwC

(vii) Seizing the Mobility Moment

June 7, 2012
   http://bit.ly/PwC_Mobile11_June2012

Abstract.   The mobile device is changing the customer experience and forcing organizations to rethink how they engage with customers and employees. This PwC paper is the first in a series exploring the opportunities and challenges posed by the rise of mobility and how companies can capitalize on them to create experiences that strengthen relationships.

Outline.

- Mobile allows for a richer, deeper, and more personal customer experience

- Mobility isn't just about technology and gadgets. It's a global shift in how we do business
- So you think it's just about communication?
- What mobile means for consumers

Excerpt. Today, it's typical to think of mobile as a channel—mostly as a powerful communications portal. But now we have to adapt that thinking to view the handset or the tablet as a single device that blends contextual awareness with personal awareness. The day is coming when the device will even serve as our personal area network, meaning that we'll sense other devices and communicate with them seamlessly—without having to look at screens or hit buttons or keys.

(viii) Manufacturing Barometer: Business Outlook Report—April 2012

May 3, 2012
    http://bit.ly/PwC_Mobile31_April2012

Abstract. With the emergence of technologies (social media, cloud computing, mobile devices), the expectations of consumers, business customers, suppliers, and employees continue to change. This impacts business models, customer strategies, and ongoing operations. This issue of *Manufacturing Barometer* reveals panelists' views on this digital transformation.

Outline.

- Special topic: Digital change and digital transformation
- How important is technology?
- Used technology to improve performance
- Effectiveness of these technology improvements
- Importance of digital change and digital transformation
- How have demands and needs of customers changed?
- How have demands and needs of suppliers/partners changed?
- Revising companies' business model?
- Implementing the following technologies
- Business benefits of digital change

(ix) Gaps in the Apps: Why the Traditional Security Lifecycle No Longer Works

April 4, 2012
    http://bit.ly/PwC_Mobile10_April2012

Abstract.   The rise of mobile payments and the rapid growth of new nonbank competitors have provided consumers with an abundance of banking alternatives and led banks into a race to develop mobile banking applications. Many banks have failed to keep pace with the design and implementation of sound security measures, leaving them vulnerable to security breaches that will prompt customers to switch financial institutions and cause reputational damage. In addition, financial services institutions are prime targets for criminals with their global operating models, data flowing to third-party service providers, and big payoffs from stolen data.

Various financial services institutions have experienced difficulty maintaining the appropriate level of security to protect against breaches. PwC supports clients in developing a mobile banking security strategy that helps to reduce security breaches while allowing for flexibility to meet future mobile security regulations, which in turn can help organizations earn and retain customer loyalty.

Excerpt.   The use of mobile banking is dramatically escalating. At the same time, the lack of strong security measures is increasing the likelihood of data breaches—making sensitive customer data a prime target for criminals and exposing financial institutions and their customers to associated risk. Case in point—in February 2012, a popular mobile payment service disabled one of its offerings after a serious security flaw was discovered. The security issue would have potentially allowed someone to access prepaid card balances stored on a lost phone. Not only was part of the mobile payment service not available to customers for several days as a fix was developed—it also left many customers wondering about the safety of the service and whether they should continue using it.

(x) Selfsumerization: Transforming the Enterprise

2012
    http://bit.ly/PwC_Mobile3_2012

Abstract.   In this thought leadership paper, we introduce and explain emerging developments in *selfsumerization* of the enterprise arising from recent great advances in electronic devices, location awareness, 3D, cloud-mobility symbiosis, high-speed networking, and the increasing presence of Generation Y in the workforce.

Selfsumerization will lead to marked changes in the next two to five years in the way that private and public sector enterprises will balance versatility, risk, productivity, and worker and client satisfaction.

Enterprise C-suites, boards of directors, employees, and clients in private and public sectors will likely find these insights thought-provoking and relevant to improving their strategies and services to increase business successes.

Outline.

- Enterprise driven by mobile selfsumer and cloud
- Serious games and 3D in the enterprise
- Social networking and selfsumer relationship management
- CIO and C-suite evolution and innovative next steps

Excerpt.   Selfsumers use their considerable laptop, tablet, and smartphone skills to engage with sources of multimedia information. They use social communication to discover, discuss and team at play and work, and view and discuss product offerings from multiple sources. They expect, if not yet demand, enterprises to provide in-company social networking and collaboration applications to increase sharing, team efficiencies, and work satisfaction.

(xi) PwC's 4th Annual Digital IQ Survey: The Mobile Consumer

2012
    http://bit.ly/PwC_Mobile26_2012

Abstract.   Executives must recognize that the expectations of employees and customers are largely affected by consumer-driven technologies. Employees want the tools they use for work to be as good as those they use in their personal lives, and customers expect to interact with firms on the platform and device of their choice. The survey shows that while many firms are focused on developing better mobile tools for their workers, they are underinvesting in solutions for their customers: Only 45 percent of all respondents say they interact with customers significantly using mobile channels, and less than one third are currently investing in mobile technologies for customers.

Excerpt.   Cybercrime is driven by ROI and, as a rule, the more popular the operating system, the more enticing it will be to hackers.

The Android OS, which currently claims 45 percent of the U.S. mobile market, is the most prevalent target for malware developers today. Android is an open-source platform that, unlike iOS or the BlackBerry operating systems, is not tightly controlled and is thereby inherently more appealing to attackers. The Apple iOS, with 27 percent U.S. market share, is considered comparatively secure, but security risks escalate when users jailbreak devices to override the limitations of the operating system. Regardless of OS, all WiFi-enabled handhelds are vulnerable to attacks that allow a hacker to commandeer a user's e-mail and social networking accounts.

(xii) Managing Security in a Mobile World

2012

    http://bit.ly/PwC_Mobile22_2012

Abstract. Employee use of mobile devices has skyrocketed, creating unprecedented threats to information security. Businesses that prepare for these risks can enhance productivity and gain competitive advantages.

Outline.

- The heart of the matter
- An in-depth discussion: How mobile devices jeopardize security
- A trifecta of ascendant risk
- How security enables effective mobility
- Taking the first steps toward a mobile strategy
- What this means for your business
- Contacts

Excerpt. As consumers fuse their personal and professional lives on one device, many have discovered that their handsets lack adequate storage. Increasingly, they are turning to consumer cloud services to store and sync information. These public cloud services are convenient, yet they jeopardize security because they are out of IT's control. Storage of corporate data on public cloud services raises concerns about data security, ownership of data, and data leakage, among others.

(xiii) Mobile Technology's Journey from Peril to Promise

2012

   http://bit.ly/PwC_Mobile21_2012

Abstract. Given the passion for mobile computing among users and the tech industry, it is easy to get swept up in the excitement and see mobile as the solution for everything. It's also not hard to write off the technology as a fad that will run its course. We're betting the first camp is more on target, given the rapid adoption of mobile technology by business users and consumers with fervor reminiscent of the early PC days.

In conversations with CIOs and other IT leaders, PwC sees a sea change in attitude toward mobile devices. Once viewed as an oddity to be kept at arm's length, they're now seen as a platform for enterprise value through their existing functions and ones not yet invented.

Excerpt. "The mobile industry has reached a point where the economics of the current subsidy model associated with acquiring new and upgrading existing customers to costly smartphones have become increasingly difficult to sustain. Customers are becoming less loyal and the average length of postpaid customer relationships has declined to 48 months in the 2011 survey, from 59 months in the 2010 survey. Carriers are revisiting their approach to customer relationships and considering new ways to retain subscribers such as device buyback initiatives, leasing programs, and 'bring your own device' approaches." —Pierre-Alain Sur, Global Communications Industry Leader, PwC

(xiv) The Consumer-Led Mobile Smartphone Transformation

December 12, 2011

   http://bit.ly/PwC_Mobile12_December2011

Abstract. Smartphones have transformed the way consumers connect with businesses and each other. For businesses, capitalizing on this transformation represents a wealth of opportunities.

This PwC report summarizes key findings from a quantitative survey and follow-up focus groups with smartphone users, exploring how consumers use smartphones, how the technology has affected their everyday lives, and how much they expect to increase their use of smartphone activities during the next few years.

Smartphones are here to stay. The challenge for companies is to determine how to use mobility to capture growth and uncover new forms of competitive advantage.

Excerpt.   The shift from PC to smartphone-based management of key activities, such as managing personal finances and health-care issues, remains critically dependent on the ability to deliver secure data management and protection. Building a competitive advantage and capturing growth in the mobile environment requires that the organization's security strategy extends fully into the mobile environment; it needs to provide end-to-end safeguards for customer profile data and transactions.

(xv) Dialing Up a Storm: How Mobile Payments Will Create the Most Significant Revenue Opportunities of the Decade for Financial Institutions

November 3, 2011
    http://bit.ly/PwC_Mobile4_November2011

Abstract.   Changes to the payments ecosystem from the advent of mobile services put more than $20 billion in play for financial services industry participants—through both new revenue opportunities and potential loss mitigation. Financial institutions have been cautious entrants into this space, leaving the door wide open for a leader to emerge and gain significant first-mover advantages.

The emerging race is resulting in new business models. For financial institutions to succeed, there are organizational changes that will be required to deliver the right operating model. This will enable them to play new roles and deliver new services in an open, collaborative, and fast-paced environment.

The question for most observers remains, "Who will be the winner in the emerging space?" Traditional players currently have an early lead; however, if they do not keep up with the fast pace of change, tech innovators and collaborators will prevail. This edition of PwC's *FS Viewpoints* explores how financial institutions should be preparing to offer the most support for their customers.

Outline.

- Current situation
- Competitive intelligence

- A framework for response
- How PwC can help

(xvi) Redefining the Customer Experience: Mobile Telematics and the Future of the Insurance Industry

January 2011
   http://bit.ly/PwC_Mobile18_January2011

Abstract.   Recent technological advancements, widespread adoption of smartphones, and the ever-evolving nature of vehicle communications systems represent a unique confluence of trends that present a significant opportunity for insurers. By incorporating mobile telematics into the core business strategy, insurers can fundamentally alter and improve the value proposition for consumers in an unprecedented way.

Outline.

- Widespread, adaptable, and affordable technologies make mobile telematics easier to develop, introduce, and support than ever before.
- Why should insurance companies care about the growth of mobile telematics?
- The traditional, reactive touch points that occur mainly after accidents could shift toward proactive, preventative interactions based on attractive add-on services.

Excerpt.   Insurers have historically turned to both integrated in-car and post-purchase telematics technology systems to support information gathering, transmission of location data, and value-added service provision. It is no secret, however, that most insurers have struggled to make telematics an integral part of their core business strategy.

   In most cases, insurers have employed a restrictively narrow strategic approach in addressing two main issues: Initially, how to recoup the cost of the telematics device or platform and, subsequently, how to create a compelling consumer value proposition that includes the sharing of driving data as the basis for pricing and underwriting. Meanwhile, insurers continue to leave on the table significant opportunities to fundamentally redefine the customer experience.

The recent evolution of smartphones and mobile applications can help insurers approach both of these long-standing problems from a very different angle—one that supports a mutually beneficial and mutually reinforcing relationship for both the consumer and insurer.

(xvii) A Look at the Future of Mobile Data

2010

http://bit.ly/PwC_Mobile13_2010

Abstract. This paper presents an overview of the current mobile data landscape for both operators and content creators. It discusses ways in which operators and content creators can position themselves to succeed with a mobile data strategy review, including critical questions to conduct a health check on their mobile data strategy and plan.

Excerpt. "Mobile operators are playing a vital role in defining and implementing a new generation of 'smart' enabling services. The operators need to work closer with the content industry to create viable business models behind these services."—Gary Schwartz, chair, North American Mobile Entertainment Forum (MEF)

Section 3: Analytics

(i) Advancing Health-Care Informatics: The Power of Partnerships

September 21, 2012

http://bit.ly/PwC_AdvancingHealthcare

Abstract. Health insurers, assuming the role of data aggregator and leveraging their technology and analytics capabilities, offer significant value to all health-care stakeholders. Early experiments in the formation of accountable care organizations, as well as the mobilization of health insurance exchanges, offer a window into how even adversaries can team up to produce better results for patients and the bottom line. Based on the Health Research Institute's in-depth spring 2012 informatics report, this PwC publication provides more insight into the opportunities for the health insurance industry.

Outline.

- Advancing health-care informatics: Insurers lead the way
- Insurers as change agent
- Forming new partnerships: One plus one equals three
- Instilling trust through experimentation: Outcomes-based reimbursement leads to more data sharing
- Aggregating the data: Insurers sharing information that improves quality of care
- Insurers casting a wider net
- Remapping care and improving the consumer experience
- What this means for your business

Excerpt. For years, data analytic strategies in the insurance world have focused on the same low-hanging fruit, spotting cost trends in claims reports. Using medical claims to identify consumers who have a diabetes diagnosis, for example, and helping them enroll in a tailored health and wellness plan is important, but it is no longer a differentiating capability. Expanding data components to include employer demographics, public/community health, and social media are examples of untapped data sources rich with consumer information, and it presents opportunities to learn from and engage with members more effectively.

(ii) Using Data to Your Advantage

March 2011
http://bit.ly/PwC_Analytics10_March2011

Abstract. Beyond the big headlines of the day, trends are emerging that will dictate how businesses leverage their own data, and the way they interact and market to existing and potential customers. This article emphasizes the importance of data and analyzing social data and examines trends and case studies.

Excerpt. "Relying on gut feelings are good for certain decisions in your business, but not for understanding your customers' behavior. You need real data and numbers to make your business the most efficient and profitable it can be." —Kevin North, CEO, Terapeak, a Vancouver-based data company.

Companies like Infochimps, Cloudera, and DataMeer are helping companies collect, analyze, and leverage their data. And this trend will only continue to grow as companies look for ways to turn their data into revenue.

(iii) Dynamic Analytics for Enhanced Business Decision Making in the Entertainment Industry

June 2012
   http://bit.ly/PwC_Analytics11_Juneof2012

Abstract.   Analytics are used increasingly throughout the entertainment and media (E&M) industry. In fact, companies that have extensively implemented analytics have used it as a differentiator and are three times as likely to outperform their competitors. This publication briefly explores the range of analytical techniques available today, presents a proposed structure for a successful analytics project, and focuses on simulation modeling as an effective tool to address E&M macro strategic decisions.

Outline.   The paper provides two case study examples:

- Feature film lifecycle simulation, which illustrates how simulation is used to forecast and optimize the revenues generated by movies across the full spectrum of release windows.
- Television content value simulation, which uses a holistic approach to simulation modeling to provide a comparative value for series-level television programming scenarios.

Excerpt.   Analytical solutions have become an important component in addressing complex and strategic issues, and are used increasingly throughout the E&M industry. In fact, companies that have extensively implemented analytics have used it as a differentiator and are three times as likely to outperform their competitors.

The industry is in a period of significant and rapid change brought about by evolving digital distribution technologies and the widening range of products and services they have engendered. This paper will briefly explore the range of analytical techniques available today, present a proposed structure for a successful analytics project, and then focus on simulation modeling as an effective tool to address E&M macro strategic decisions in a rapidly changing world.

(iv) The Third Wave of Customer Analytics

April 2012
    http://bit.ly/PwC_Analytics4_April2012

Abstract.   This issue of *Technology Forecast* explores the impact of the new analytics and this culture of inquiry. This first article examines the essential ingredients of the new analytics, using several examples. The other articles in this issue focus on the technologies behind these capabilities (see the article, "The Art and Science of New Analytics Technology") and identify the main elements of a CIO strategic framework for effectively taking advantage of the full range of analytics capabilities (see the article, "How CIOs Can Build the Foundation for a Data Science Culture").

Outline.

- Introduction
- More computing speed, storage, and ability to scale
- More time and better tools
- More data sources
- More focus on key metrics
- Better access to results
- Conclusion: A broader culture of inquiry

Excerpt.   The technology trends behind FT.com's improvements in advertising operations—more accessible data; faster, less-expensive computing; new software tools; and improved user interfaces— are driving a new era in analytics use at large companies around the world, in which enterprises make decisions with a precision comparable to scientific insight. The new analytics use a rigorous scientific method, including hypothesis formation and testing, with science-oriented statistical packages and visualization tools. It is spawning business unit "data scientists" who are replacing the centralized analytics units of the past. These trends will accelerate, and business leaders who embrace the new analytics will be able to create cultures of inquiry that lead to better decisions throughout their enterprises.

(v) The Art and Science of New Analytics Technology

February 2012
    http://bit.ly/PwC_ArtAndScienceOfNewAnalyticsTechnology

Abstract.   This article explores some of the newer technologies that make feasible the case studies and the evolving cultures of inquiry described in "The Third Wave of Customer Analytics." These technologies include the following:

- **In-memory technology.** Reducing response time and expanding the reach of business intelligence (BI) by extending the use of main (random access) memory
- **Interactive visualization.** Merging the user interface and the presentation of results into one responsive visual analytics environment
- **Statistical rigor.** Bringing more of the scientific method and evidence into corporate decision making
- **Associative search.** Navigating to specific names and terms by browsing the nearby context

Outline.

- Introduction
- In-memory technology
- Self-service BI and interactive visualization
- Bringing more statistical rigor to business decisions
- Conclusion: No lack of vision, resources, or technology

Excerpt.   The new analytics are the art and science of turning the invisible into the visible. It's about finding "unknown unknowns," as former U.S. secretary of defense Donald Rumsfeld famously called them, and learning at least something about them. It's about detecting opportunities and threats you hadn't anticipated, or finding people you didn't know existed who could be your next customers. It's about learning what's really important, rather than what you thought was important. It's about identifying, committing, and following through on what your enterprise must change most.

(vi) Natural Language Processing and Social Media Intelligence

February 2012
   http://bit.ly/PwC_Social6_February2012

Abstract.   Most enterprises are more than eager to further develop their capabilities in social media intelligence (SMI)—the ability to mine the public social media cloud to glean business insights and act on them. They understand the essential value of finding customers who discuss products and services candidly in public forums. The impact SMI can have goes beyond basic market research and test marketing. In the best cases, companies can uncover clues to help them revisit product and marketing strategies.

This article explores the primary characteristics of natural language processing (NLP), which is the key to SMI, and how NLP is applied to social media analytics. The article considers what's in the realm of the possible when mining social media text, and how informed human analysis becomes essential when interpreting the conversations that machines are attempting to evaluate.

Outline.

- Natural language processing: Its components and social media applications
- NLP-related best practices
- Conclusion: A machine-assisted and iterative process, rather than just processing alone

Excerpt. "Ideally, social media can function as a really big focus group. Enterprises, which spend billions on focus groups, spent nearly $1.6 billion in 2011 on social media marketing, according to Forrester Research. That number is expected to grow to nearly $5 billion by 2016." —Jeff Auker, a Director, Customer Impact Practice, PwC.

(vii) Putting Predictive Analytics to Work

January 2012
    http://bit.ly/PwC_Analytics3_January2012

Abstract. If your company is ready to leverage predictive analytics for a specific problem or decision, first ask yourselves: What will the cost be to our company if management makes a wrong business decision? What types of business decisions are we looking to inform with predictive data? Is there a correct tool we should plan on using? The answers to these and other key questions will help you identify and successfully engineer a solution to your company's specific analytic goals. The information garnered during this process will contribute, in large part, to a how-to guide that will serve as a strong foundation on which to build your company-specific predictive analytics initiative.

Outline.

- Predictive analytics: Businesses want to do it, but few know where to begin
- Asking the right questions up front is a keystone of success
- Companies that do their homework can reap multiple benefits

Excerpt.   In our experience, successful decision delivery is challenging, as it requires cross-organizational coordination among the analytics, business, and IT groups to ensure that information lands in the hands of the decision maker at the point of decision. The job of the analytics group is to make their analysis results relevant to the decision maker's workflow. This could take the form of a mobile handheld device for a distributed sales force, customer relationship management (CRM) systems integration for call centers, or an executive dashboard for reporting system integration.

(viii) Reshaping the Workforce with the New Analytics

2012, Issue 1
   http://bit.ly/PwC_ReshapingTheWorkforce

Abstract.   This issue of *Technology Forecast* examines advanced analytics through this lens of increasing instrumentation. PwC's view is that the flow of data at this new, more complete level of resolution travels in an arc beginning with big data techniques (including NoSQL and in-memory databases), through advanced statistical packages (from the traditional SPSS and SAS to open source offerings such as R), to analytic visualization tools that put interactive graphics in the control of business unit specialists. This arc is positioning the enterprise to establish a new culture of inquiry, where decisions are driven by analytical precision that rivals scientific insight.

Outline.

- **The third wave of customer analytics.** Today, there's only one way to scale the analysis of customer-related information to increase sales and profits—by tapping the data and human resources of the extended enterprise.

- **The art and science of new analytics technology.** Left-brain analysis connects with right-brain creativity.
- **Natural language processing and social media intelligence.** Mining insights from social media data requires more than sorting and counting words.
- **How CIOs can build the foundation for a data science culture.** Helping to establish a new culture of inquiry can be a way for these executives to reclaim a leadership role in information.

Interviews.

- Mike Driscoll of Metamarkets discusses how cloud analytics are improving query speed
- Jon Slade of the *Financial Times* discusses the benefits of cloud analytics for online ad placement and pricing.
- Jock Mackinlay of Tableau Software describes how more of the workforce can become engaged in analytics
- Ashwin Rangan of Edwards Lifesciences details what's different about hemodynamic monitoring methods these days
- Arvind Parthasarathi of YarcData describes the emerging field of relationship analytics

Excerpt. "In the middle of looking at some data, you can change your mind about what question you're asking. You need to be able to head toward that new question on the fly No automated system is going to keep up with the stream of human thought."—Jock Mackinlay, Director of Visual Analysis, Tableau Software, one of the vendors of the new visualization front ends for analytics.

(ix) Data Analytics: How Data Analytics Can Help Internal Audit Better Understand Risk

2012

http://bit.ly/PwC_Analytics7_2012

Abstract. Internal audit departments have a unique opportunity to leverage data analytics to identify risks and provide insights to the business. While it is management's responsibility to ensure that risks are appropriately mitigated, internal audit can focus its use of data analytics to hone in on areas or transactions where controls do not exist or are not operating effectively.

Excerpt. With the advent of advanced billing systems, a deep CIS skill set can allow internal audit to mine billing data to identify operational trends leading to credits, cancelled or recalculated bills; pinpoint billing errors; and independently assess key incentive metrics. In wholesale trading, data analytics can be used to confirm trader limits, and patterns within certain trades not monitored by deal trade systems. Data analytics can also be used to mine for cost recovery in contract compliance related to capital spend. These reviews can sometimes partially or fully underwrite the cost of the analytics by identifying recoverable costs.

(x) How CIOs Can Build the Foundation for a Data Science Culture

November 2011
    http://bit.ly/PwC_CIOsAndNewAnalyticsMovement

Abstract. The new analytics requires that CIOs and IT organizations find new ways to engage with their business partners. For all the strategic opportunities new analytics offer the enterprise, it also threatens the relevance of the CIO. The threat comes from the fact that the CIO's business partners are being sold data analytics services and software outside normal IT procurement channels, which cuts out of the process the very experts who can add real value. The new analytics needs to be treated as a long-term collaboration between IT and business partners—similar to the relationship PwC has advocated (see the article "The Consumerization of IT: The Next-Generation CIO," referenced earlier in Appendix) for the general consumerization-of-IT phenomenon invoked by mobility, social media, and cloud services. This tight collaboration can be a win for the business and for the CIO. The new analytics is a chance for the CIO to shine, reclaim the "I" leadership in CIO, and provide a solid footing for a new culture of inquiry.

Outline.

- Introduction
- The many ways for CIOs to be new analytics leaders
- Enable the data scientist

- Renew the IT infrastructure for the new analytics
- Develop the new analytics strategic plan
- Provision data, tools, and infrastructure
- Update IT capabilities: Leverage the cloud's capacity
- Conclusion

Excerpt. Because most enterprises have been frustrated by the lack of clear payoffs from large investments in data analysis, they may be tempted to treat the new analytics as not really new. This would be a mistake. As with most developments in IT, there is something old, something new, something borrowed, and possibly something blue in the new analytics. Not everything is new, but that doesn't justify treating the new analytics as more of the same. In fact, doing so indicates that your adoption of the new analytics is merely applying new tools and perhaps personnel to your existing activities. It's not the tool per se that solves problems or finds insights—it's the people who are able to explore openly and freely and to think outside the box, aided by various tools. So don't just re-create or refurbish the existing box.

(xi) Approaches in Valuing BPO Companies

September 2011
    http://bit.ly/PwC_Analytics9_September2011

Abstract. Chief executive officers or owners who wish to sell or buy a business must be armed with a sound knowledge of its value in order to put a profitable price tag on the firm. Otherwise, what would be their basis for negotiations? Or some may simply want to know what their company is worth.

This article enumerates the methods that are employed in business valuation. It also describes the combination of methods that were used to determine a business process outsourcing company's worth.

(xii) Using Analytics to Get the Most from Your Transaction Monitoring System

March 2011
    http://bit.ly/PwC_Analytics8_March2011

Abstract. Through a bounty of legislation, financial institutions must identify and report customer money laundering activity, or face stiff penalties. That's why institutions charged with this responsibility must have a program in place that continually evaluates performance and incorporates triggers to identify areas of risk and procedures for mitigating that risk. This document discusses how such a program can help financial institutions facilitate the examination process, pro-actively address areas of likely regulatory focus, and contribute to cost reduction.

Outline.

- Components of the anti-money laundering (AML) compliance program
- Transaction monitoring
- Transaction monitoring performance enhancement
- Structure of performance enhancement efforts
- Determining the approach

Excerpt. Ultimately, the decision about the type and extent of transaction monitoring performance enhancement efforts depends on an evaluation of the compliance and business risks inherent in the monitoring system, regulatory and legal requirements, and available resources. Having a program in place that continually evaluates performance and incorporates triggers to identify areas of risk and procedures for mitigating risk will facilitate the examination process, proactively address areas of likely regulatory focus, and contribute to cost reduction. Key to this effort is having staff that is trained in implementing the various statistical techniques, as well as AML analysts who can assist in interpreting the results that are being generated from the performance enhancement efforts.

Section 4: Cloud

(i) Technology Forecast: The Business Value of APIs

Issue 2, March 2012
    http://bit.ly/PwC_Cloud8_March2012

Abstract. The business value of APIs examines how enterprises can engage with the challenges and opportunities stemming from SMAC trends by scaling integrations and participating in expanding digital ecosystems.

Outline.

- The article "Exploiting the Growing Value from Information," on page 6 examines how creating open interfaces to engage a growing digital ecosystem will empower enterprises to build a digital operating model and progress toward becoming a permeable enterprise.
- "Consumerization of APIs" on page 34 explains why a new generation of tools based on RESTful APIs scales the ability to make digital connections by sharply reducing the cost and complexity of integrations in digital ecosystems.
- The article, "Embracing open IT," on page 54 examines how, by positioning IT capabilities as a platform composed of open, self-describing, modular services, CIOs can manage challenges from SMAC and enable the permeable enterprise.

Interviews.

- John Donovan, Sanjay Macwan, and Jacob Feinstein of AT&T detail how the API program is a driver of speed in their innovation efforts.
- David Zanca and Thomas Wicinski of FedEx Services describe how FedEx is a connected enterprise and provides digital access to its services on the customer's terms.
- Mark Noworolski and Peter Leiser of Streetline detail how they are transforming the parking ecosystem with cloud, mobility, and analytics technologies using RESTful APIs.
- Sam Ramji of Apigee explains why APIs are of strategic importance to all businesses.
- Devon Biondi of Mashery details how APIs allow businesses to engage with customers in their context.
- Laura Merling and John Musser of Alcatel-Lucent share how enterprises can use APIs to create platforms from existing assets to unlock new value.
- Brian Katz of Sanofi discusses how consumerization of IT means enterprise IT should treat users as partners.

Excerpt.   Social computing scales business collaboration from a few to hundreds or thousands of others. Mobile computing scales process and data management into almost any business context. Advanced analytics—with big data, terabytes of in-memory databases, and visualization—scales business intelligence into every aspect of business operations. And cloud computing promises more compute power than ever before. These disruptions are all delivered over digital networks as digital services, usually from outside the enterprise. For many business and IT executives, the potential value of engaging with these four trends is transparent. The challenge is scaling their integration with traditional IT. In the best of circumstances, internal legacy systems integrate well with each other. But they rarely were designed to rapidly integrate with digitally delivered external services.

(ii) Cloud Computing and the Role of the CHRO

December 7, 2012
   http://bit.ly/PwC_Cloud10_December2012

Abstract. This article emphasizes the following points:

- Cloud computing can reduce human capital management (HCM) costs, and it is fast becoming a powerful engine for growth.
- Cloud solutions will enable chief human resource officers (CHROs) to focus on new strategies and value-adding innovations for human resources (HR).
- The CHRO should set expectations for cloud services needs, costs, and vendor offerings.
- Cloud computing will require that CHROs lead and manage change across the entire organization.

Excerpt. Many CHROs have adopted cloud computing to help meet these challenges. Cloud applications enable you to quickly implement cost-effective capabilities and streamline HR processes. Best-of-breed features enable cloud-based talent management solutions to provide a comprehensive view into employee performance that empowers HR and business leaders to quickly make informed human capital decisions. They also can promote innovation and collaboration across divisions by leveraging social media and networking tools, which are critical to attracting the next generation of young workers. And the economies of scale inherent in a shared server environment contribute to a sustainable approach to IT, a corporate commitment that is increasingly vital to a company's brand.

(iii) Storing Entertainment Content in the Cloud

March 30, 2012
   http://bit.ly/PwC_Cloud15_march2012

Abstract.   Amid the recent launch of music, photo, and video content services, consumers appear to be more informed about digital lockers yet consumers still lack a strong understanding of the benefits of digital lockers or the rights that come with ownership. This report includes quantitative findings from an online survey of 502 participants and findings from a number of focus groups where PwC explored consumers' awareness, interest, and engagement with digital content storage, including their willingness to pay for it. Ultimately, the success of digital lockers will depend on whether companies can match the benefits with consumers' desires—and ensuring consumers fully understand the value of digital lockers for all types of content.

(iv) Navigating the Cloud

February 23, 2012
   http://bit.ly/PwC_Cloud11_February2012

Abstract.   Based on a survey of more than 50 cloud services providers in Germany, this PwC report demonstrates how these providers are meeting current demand and identifies their most significant risks and opportunities. The quantitative data is supported with comments taken from in-depth interviews with 10 executives in the German cloud space. While the survey is conducted solely among German cloud service providers, the challenges and opportunities explored are relevant the world over.

Outline.

- Summary
- Background
- The results of the survey
  - Contract creation
  - Data migration
  - Risks and compliance
  - Data protection
  - Information security
  - Outlook

- Methodology
- Demographics: Cloud services providers

Excerpt. Cloud computing enables companies to procure their IT resources over the Internet—on a flexible basis, cost efficiently, almost limitlessly, and effectively with payment based on consumption. This means that companies no longer need to keep a certain amount of computer capacity or data storage space free, or constantly run applications. This leads to a reduction of necessary capacity, investments, and costs for companies, and, most important, allows them to structure their specialist departments in new ways.

(v) Why CIOs Need to Be Ahead of the Game

December 2011
    http://bit.ly/PwC_Cloud9_December2011

Abstract. The key to having cloud be a value-added part of your organizational framework is to develop a sound strategy at the outset. Today's business leaders are increasingly using the cloud to transform their capabilities and gain business agility and competitive advantage. But what are the implications for public sector agencies and government organizations? And what should public sector CIOs consider when preparing for this dynamic business trend? This paper is designed to help you on your journey as you select and develop your cloud solution.

Outline.

- Explaining cloud computing and the various deployment and service models
- Highlighting the implications of cloud on the public sector (perceived barriers and benefits)
- Reviewing the public sector experience to date in various jurisdictions around the world
- Outlining an approach to developing a cloud computing strategy

Excerpt. Creating a cloud strategy begins by establishing a baseline. Consider all aspects of cloud computing with your executive team: the challenges you're facing as business leaders; the sourcing solutions that the cloud can deliver to meet those challenges; the related risks, potential rewards and the impact of each option; and the overall business goals of the enterprise. This will help to reach agreement on the key components and objectives of your cloud sourcing strategy.

(vi) The Next Generation of Cloud Computing

November 22, 2011
  http://bit.ly/PwC_Cloud12_November2011

Abstract.   When discussing moving to the cloud, the question has become "how and how fast" rather than "why." In the new era of cloud computing, the CIO will take the role and responsibilities of a cloud broker, controlling the sourcing, implementation, and management of multiple cloud services. The CIO must assess the organization's needs to identify business opportunities that will drive revenue and competitive advantage, and then develop an integrated strategy that may include public, private, and hybrid cloud services. At all times, the CIO must anticipate potential information security issues. It is, to be sure, a challenging role.

But when coupled with a CIO's IT strategy around data center transformation, service virtualization, and unified fabrics, cloud computing offers synergies that can bring a new order of competitive advantage. Forward-thinking CIOs must be prepared to lead their organization into the cloud. Doing so can create an accelerated trajectory to success—for the CIO and for the entire organization.

Outline.

- Challenges to cloud computing
- Despite maturity, some confusion lingers
- The power of partnering
- How the CIO can lead innovation

Excerpt.   CIOs are troubled by potential damage to reputation and revenue as a result of service downtime. High-profile incidents affecting leading cloud providers in recent months have done little to allay fears. Although uptime and resilience may never be 100 percent guaranteed, CIOs can help ensure uptime by pursuing high availability options and ensuring traditional disaster recovery plans are in place to mitigate potential downtime whether it is in the cloud or the enterprise.

(vii) Cloud Overview

October 2011
http://bit.ly/PwC_CloudComputing2_October2011

Abstract. This document contains information on PwC's service offerings, including enabling cloud infrastructure, transforming business operations, and developing differentiated services. It also covers channels to market the cloud computing services and highlights PwC's differentiators.

Outline.

- Service offerings
  - Enabling cloud infrastructure
  - Transforming business operations
  - Developing differentiated services
- Channels to market
- Differentiators

(viii) The Future of IT Outsourcing and Cloud Computing

Spring 2011
http://bit.ly/PwC_CloudComputing3_Spring2011

Abstract. For all the hype about cloud computing, there is very little survey data on the extent enterprises are planning for and adopting cloud computing as a replacement for traditional data center infrastructure technologies and management processes. PwC surveyed 489 business executives to find answers to these and other questions about the state of data center infrastructure management. Individual interviews with vendors offering traditional ITO and new cloud-based offerings, including infrastructure as a service (IaaS), complemented the survey. We sought to understand the real state of data center management today, how fast business executives expect to move to cloud infrastructures in the future, and who they will turn to—traditional ITO providers, new cloud-oriented providers, or internal staff—to make the shift. Finally, what is the bigger goal, a shift to public cloud offerings or a transition to private clouds? This series of articles and graphics examines and interprets these trends.

Outline.

- Introduction, survey methodology, and demographics
- Article 1—Infrastructure as a service: new providers innovate to win enterprise cloud business
- Article 2—The ITO challenge: Providers must offer both cloud and traditional IT services
- Article 3—The big dilemma: Security versus scalability in the public cloud
- Article 4—Cloud value proposition: Little consensus on how the cloud will benefit enterprises
- Article 5—Big cloud hurdle: Workload readiness is the key to accelerating cloud adoption
- Article 6—Similarities and differences: ITO customers and non-customers seek somewhat different cloud services
- Conclusion—A cloudy future

Excerpt.   "We have seen major technology shifts in the data center in the past. These shifts in reality have just added to the mix in the data center, increasing complexity and cost. Cloud computing, when done right, has the potential to actually replace, and not just augment, legacy environments while adding value by reducing costs and increasing agility."—David Stuckey, Leader of Data Center Infrastructure Practice, PWC

Do enterprises see it that way? Are they making plans? Who do they take advice from? What business advantages are they anticipating?

(ix) Exploring the Potential of the Cloud—The New Sourcing Alternative

April 19, 2011
    http://bit.ly/PwC_ExplorePotentialofCloud

Abstract.   Cloud computing—a dynamic business trend—is increasing its penetration into the business realm. Cloud computing is not just a better IT solution; it's a better business solution—one that addresses the critical challenges facing today's C-suite executives such as accelerating business innovation, facilitating delivery of more personalized services, improving employee productivity, and optimizing the total cost of technology.

The careful sourcing of IT—infrastructure and applications— which PwC refers to as cloud sourcing can empower enterprises to simplify their infrastructure and potentially reduce costs by standardizing platforms and introducing new skills and management practices. As a result, we are seeing leading organizations scaling back on traditional IT service delivery to leverage the benefits of the cloud. This paper describes the issues companies need to consider and the steps they need to take to develop a cloud sourcing strategy.

Outline.

- Exploring the potential of the cloud—a new sourcing alternative
- An in-depth discussion
- Leveraging the power of cloud sourcing
- What this means for your business
- Reaping the benefits of infrastructure-free IT services

Excerpt. As companies are faced with ever-higher operating and capital expenditures, cloud sourcing provides an alternate sourcing model for CIOs and IT leaders. When strategically thought through in terms of risks and rewards, and then carefully implemented and well-managed over time, cloud computing has the potential to meet C-suite challenges by accelerating business innovation, meeting growing user demand for individual- and location-centric services, improving employee productivity, and optimizing the organization's total cost of technology.

(x) Protecting Your Brand in the Cloud: Transparency and Trust through Enhanced Reporting

January 20, 2011
   http://bit.ly/PwC_TransparencyAndTrust

Abstract. As organizations consider moving key business processes and IT infrastructure to cloud computing, they are concerned about risks. They are right to be concerned. In moving to the cloud, companies give up significant control over security, privacy, availability, and data protection and retention. A problem in any one of these areas could damage a company's business—and its brand.

This PwC paper explores how cloud risks could negatively impact companies' brands. Many cloud providers are working to address risks with strong controls, but these providers lack a trusted way to demonstrate the adequacy of their infrastructures to potential customers. Third-party assurance may be the answer for both cloud users and providers. With third-party assurance, a trusted third party evaluates and reports on a cloud provider's ability to deliver promised levels of service and protection from risk.

Outline.

- Establishing trust in cloud computing
- Risks with cloud computing
- Protecting against risks with an independent perspective

Excerpt.   IT is on the brink of a radical transformation—the movement of software, platforms, and infrastructure to the cloud. As cloud computing takes hold, it will change the way businesses think about virtually every aspect of IT. In the simplest terms, cloud computing enables businesses to use the Internet and outside service providers to store data and run processes. In-house IT costs go down even as business flexibility increases thanks to the on-demand nature of cloud computing. Increasingly, cloud computing is becoming a foundation for benefits well beyond IT cost savings—business agility fueled by rapid technology innovations will enable the digital transformation of processes.

(xi) Driving Growth with Cloud Computing

2010, Issue 4
    http://bit.ly/PwC_CloudComputing6_2010Issue4

Abstract.   This issue of *Technology Forecast* covers the cloud-computing phenomenon not from a how or where perspective but from a starting assumption of yes, cloud computing is becoming the IT fabric of the future. What should CEOs, CIOs, and CFOs do with it beyond making IT perform better? The first article addresses this question from the CEO's perspective, describing the extensible-enterprise concept and what it takes to become one. The second article describes the changing role of CIOs as CEOs engage with the extensible-enterprise concept. And the third article describes the impact all this will have on the CFO.

Interviews.

- Mike Capone and Jan Siegmund of Automatic Data Processing (ADP) discuss the importance of integration among ecosystem partners in creating end-customer value.
- Adam Selipsky of Amazon Web Services (AWS) describes the origins of AWS and the role modular services play in a cloud-oriented business model.
- Sanjay Mirchandani of EMC Corporation forecasts how cloud computing is changing the conversation with the business and can deliver a long-term strategic impact.
- Jaushin Lee and Andrew Wahl of Imera Systems share how virtualization of security can lead to on-demand provisioning of deep integration among ecosystem participants.
- Gary Hagmueller of Zuora details his company's journey to take the internal capability of billing and create a service in the cloud for others to build on.

Excerpt. Double-digit unemployment would seem to spell trouble for a payroll services provider, but ADP managed through the recession with flat revenues. How did it do that? Cloud computing was a key factor. Most media coverage—you've probably seen some—has focused on how the cloud makes IT less expensive and more agile. ADP has improved the efficiency of its IT organization by using the cloud, but the bigger payoff—and what helped the company avoid declining revenue—has been ADP's use of the cloud as a strategic new business development and deployment platform.

(xii) Cloud Computing Overview

March 2010
    http://bit.ly/PwC_CloudComputing1_March2010

Abstract. Case studies that document corporate clients' use of cloud technology.

Outline.

- Computer Associates Inc.
- Microsoft Inc.
- IBM
- Oracle Inc.
- Salesforce.com
- SAP AG
- Verizon
- Erich Clementi and Irving Wladawsky-Berger of IBM emphasize how standardization and mass customization principles will reduce complexity and industrialize the IT function.
- Simon Crosby of Citrix describes how virtualization creates the separation between the layers of the IT stack necessary for Evergreen IT.
- Kirill Sheynkman of Elastra explains how the intelligent software he is building will model and automate data center operations.
- Russ Daniels of EDS, an HP company, shares his insights about how IT needs to move from a build-to-order culture to a configure-to-order culture.
- Doug Hauger of Microsoft notes how cloud computing represents a technology and business model shift.

Excerpt.   Enterprise computing today is much like the early days of railways. Computing environments are purposely built collections of technology dedicated to individual workloads. Individual pieces might be "standard," but the overall environment is one of a kind. Cloud computing offers relief. But not as you might expect, given all the press devoted to external cloud services. Enterprises need to learn the lessons of logistics standardization and modularization. Doing so will empower IT to deliver much higher responsiveness and greater financial flexibility to the business.

About the Author

Ted Shelton, managing director, PwC Advisory, leads a social business consulting team focusing on the consumer, retail, and high-tech industries with PwC's Management Consulting Practice. He is an active blogger and industry thought leader on how corporations can better utilize social media and mobile technologies to manage and improve their brands, providing a deep understanding of the leading technology players currently changing the landscape of customer engagement for corporate America. He spent more than 20 years working in product development, marketing, and as a senior executive in both private and public companies as a social media-focused consultant working with clients including Alcatel-Lucent, General Motors, and Thomas Reuters on social business models for innovation and building market ecosystems. He has served as chief strategy officer of Borland Software and senior VP of sales for WhoWhere (acquired by Lycos) as well as several software and Internet start-up companies.

Index

Page numbers in *italics* refer to exhibits.

Acceptance (ADAPT concept),
    21, 53–58
Action
    PHAME concept, 99–103
    SAFE concept, 149–151
ADAPT (Awareness, Denial,
    Acceptance, Progress,
    Transformation), 53–58
    acceptance stage, 21, 55
    adaptability, and decision
        making, 151–153, 157
    adaptability, seven steps to,
        155–157
    awareness stage, 54
    denial stage, 14–15, 54–55
    Internet history and, 9
    progress stage, 55
    SAFE concept and, 150–151
    technological change, 53–54
    transaction cost economics
        and, 56–58
    transformation stage, 55–56
    See also Change
Airline industry
    flexible workforce of,
        109–110
    loyalty programs, 85
Ambient intelligence, 145–146

Analytics
    analytics-driven dashboard, 48,
        115
    data-driven decision making,
        97–103
    data mining, 48
    data storage, 45–47, 49
    data visualization technology,
        145–146, 147–148
    embracing, for adaptability, 156
Application programming
    interfaces (APIs), 46, 68
Apps
    as currency, 89–91
    gamification for employees,
        93–97
    innovation of, 11, 37
Augmented reality, 35–36,
    40–41
Awareness (ADAPT concept),
    53–58

Book publishing industry,
    e-books and, 17–18,
    120–121
Branding, by individuals, 33
"Bring your own device"
    (BYOD), 43–44, 109

Business networks
   fractalization and, 49–50
   gamification in supply chain,
      102
   personal and business online
      presence, 32–34
   utilizing, 30–32
Business plan, decision making
   for, 153–154

Call centers, 109
Change
   for continuous learning,
      137–139
   creative destruction, 121–122,
      122
   defensiveness and, 124, 132–
      134
   embracing technology and,
      14–15
   expectation and, 124, 134–135
   habit and, 124–126, 131
   identity and, 124, 126–131, 138
   overcoming self-doubt for,
      124, 134–136
   punctuated equilibrium, 119,
      120–121
   resistance to, 123, 155
   skills for success and, 136–137
   social mobile cloud and, 1–4
   systems thinking and, 143–144
   technological change, 53–54
Chief information officer (CIO)
   role
   cloud capabilities and, 50
   digital transformation and,
      18–19
   networked information
      business model and, 75–77
Choices, intention and, 144–145

Chunking, 141–144
Cloud. *See* Social mobile cloud
Co-creation ecosystems
   crowd sourcing and, 71–73
   defined, 11
   social networks and, 28–29
Collaboration
   co-creation ecosystems, 11,
      28–29, 71–73
   employee-employer
      relationship, 110–111
   understanding power of, 156
Communication
   for business, 26
   chief information officer
      (CIO) role, 18–19, 50, 75–77
   cost of, 3–4
   networked information
      business model, 75–77
   problem solving and, 57–58
   setting communication policy,
      26, 34
   social networks and
      coordination, 24
   with supply chain, 25, 27, 47
   workplace change and, 105–107
Connectivity, mobile devices for,
   35–36, 38–40
Consumption
   consumer behavior and
      smartphones, 79–82
   customer service, 61
   dynamic networked social
      sales and support staff,
      107–110
   gamification in marketplace,
      102–103
   improving, 2
   innovation and customer
      input, 11–12

IT consumerization, 43–44, 77, 109

persistent digital engagement and, 59–63

retailer as customer agent, 81–82

social networks and, 30–32

Corporate-sponsored currency

delivery system for, 83–85

loyalty programs as, 85–87

Creative destruction, 121–122, *122*

Crowd sourcing, 71–73

Currency. *See* MONEY 2.0

Cyborg, defined, 42–43

Dashboard, analytics-driven, 48, 115

Data

analytics-driven dashboard, 48, 115

data-driven decision making, 97–103

data mining, 48

data storage, 45–47, 49

data visualization technology, 145–146, 147–148

embracing, for adaptability, 156

Decision making

adaptability and, 151–153, 157

for business plan, 153–154

co-creation and, 72–73

communication and problem solving, 57–58

data-driven, for experimentation, 97–103

SAFE (Spend, Act, Foundation, Evolve), 149–153

systems thinking for, 141–148

Defensiveness (HIDE concept), 124, 132–134

Denial (ADAPT concept), 53–58

Digital kinesthesia, 32

Digital transformation

building business for social mobile cloud, 15–16

cloud as infrastructure, 18–20

Internet as business model for, 12–15

Internet history and, 9–12

merging of technology for, 7–9

smartphone importance and, 8, 20–21

speed of, 17–18

timing and, 16–17

Digitization, 65–69

Discoverability, 28

Dot-com bubble, 12

E-books, 17–18, 120–121

"Edge" devices. *See* Mobile technology

Employee-employer relationship, 105–115

changes in, 105–107

collaboration, 110–111

dynamic networked social sales and support staff, 107–110

fractalization, 49–50

games as incentive, 93–97, 99–103

transparency and openness, 111–115

Evolving, for decision making (SAFE concept), 149–153

Expectation (HIDE concept), 124, 134–136

"Experience Co-Creation" (Gouillart), 71–72

Experiment (PHAME concept),
    99–103

Fear of failure, overcoming, 124,
    134–136
Financial issues. *See*
    Consumption; MONEY 2.0
Foundation, for decision
    making (SAFE concept),
    149–151
Fractalization
    of marketplace, 49–50
    of workplace, 112–113

Gamification, 93–104
    accepting change and, 55
    currency and, 86
    data-driven decision making,
        97–103
    experience as motivation for,
        103–104
    games, defined, 95–97
    social gaming, 97
    work as game, 93–97
Generative systems. *See*
    Co-creation ecosystems
Global positioning system (GPS),
    65
Goals, for systems thinking,
    143–144, 146, 148
Gouillart, Francis, 71–72

Habit (HIDE concept), 124–126,
    131
Harvard Business Review, 71–72
HIDE (Habit, Identity,
    Defensiveness, Expectation)
    defensiveness, 132–134
    defined, 124
    expectation, 134–135
    habit, 124–126, 131
    identity, 126–131, 138
    SAFE concept and, 150–151
Hierarchy, of organizations,
    75–78
Hypothesis (PHAME concept),
    99–103

Identity (HIDE concept), 124,
    126–131, 138
Incentive design, 93–97, 99–103
Information. *See* Communication;
    Information technology (IT)
Information technology (IT)
    cloud capabilities and, 50
    consumerization of, 43–44,
        77, 109
    digital transformation and,
        18–19
Innovation
    building business for social
        mobile cloud, 15–16
    of computer industry, 37
    drivers of, 66
    importance of, 10–12
    improving, 2
Insurance, for corporate-
    sponsored currency, 87–88
Intention, 144–145
Internet
    as business model, 12–15
    history of, 9–12
    online sales competing with
        brick-and-mortar retailers,
        19, 79–82
    persistent digital engagement,
        59–63

Kinesthesia
    digital, 32

simulated kinetics and games, 98–99

Labor, erosion of jobs in, 107, 127–128
Law enforcement industry, sophisticated sensors used by, 41–42
Learning, resisting, 156–157. *See also* Change
Loyalty
corporate-sponsored currency and loyalty programs, 85–87
retailer as customer agent, 81–82 (*See also* Procurement)
Ludd, Ned, 127
Luddites, 127, 129

Manufacturer's representative, retailer as, 80
Marketplace. *See* Consumption
Metrics, PHAME concept, 99–103
Mobile payment systems, 31–32
corporate-sponsored currency, 83–91
MONEY 2.0, 82–85
Mobile technology, 35–44
augmented reality and, 35–36, 40–41
"bring your own device" (BYOD) and consumerization of IT, 43–44, 109
cloud computing with, 19
connectivity and, 35–36, 38–40
extending physical capability with, 42–43
mobile, defined, 8

persistent digital engagement of, 35–36, 38–40
sophisticated sensors and, 35–36, 41–42
technical capabilities of, 36–37
See also Smartphones
MONEY 2.0
corporate-sponsored currency, 83–91
cost of communication, 3–4
gamification and virtual currency, 93–97
mobile payment systems, 31–32
smartphones for, 82–85
Moore's Law, 36
Motivation, gamification for, 96–97, 103–104

Newspaper industry, classified advertising and, 10

Openness
in employee-employer relationship, 111–115
importance of, 11–12
of social networks, 33
Organizational antibodies, 54

Persistent digital engagement
connectivity as, 35–36, 38–40
consumption and, 59–63
defined, 2–3
gamification and, 103–104
Personal digital assistants (PDAs), 36–37
PHAME (Problem, Hypothesis, Action, Metrics, Experiment), 99–103
Physical capability, extending with mobile devices, 42–43

"Plork," 20
Point of sale, 61–62
Political campaigns, call centers
    of, 109
Power of Co-Creation, The
    (Gouillart), 71–72
Printing press, advent of, 53–54
Problem solving
    finding business model
        solutions, 77–78
    PHAME (Problem,
        Hypothesis, Action, Metrics,
        Experiment), 99–103
    See also Decision making
Procurement, 79–91
    business model solutions for,
        75
    consumer behavior, 79–82
        (*See also* Consumption)
    corporate currencies, 85–88
    mobile payment, accepting,
        88–91
    smartphone payment, 82–85
Production, improving, 2
Progress (ADAPT concept),
    53–58
Punctuated equilibrium, 119,
    120–121

"Remote control." *See*
    Smartphones
Results-oriented work
    environment, 114–115
Reward systems. *See*
    Gamification; MONEY 2.0

SAFE (Spend, Act, Foundation,
    Evolve), 149–153
Schumpeter, Joseph, 121
Security, of social networks, 34

Self-doubt, overcoming, 124,
    134–136
Sensors. *See* Sophisticated sensors
Serendipity, 28, 31, 48
Servers, cloud computing and,
    45–47
Sharing, social mobile cloud for,
    17
Smartphones
    for currency, 82–85
        (*See also* MONEY 2.0)
    digital transformation and, 8,
        11, 20–21
    fractalization of workplace,
        113
    importance of, 8
    as innovation driver, 66
    online sales competing with
        brick-and-mortar retailers,
        79–82 (*See also*
        Consumption;
        Procurement)
    persistent digital engagement
        of, 38–40 (*See also* Mobile
        technology)
    as "remote controls," 9
    social network connection
        through, 27
    systems thinking with, 144–145
Social gaming, 97
Social media, 23–34
    being connected through,
        23
    business network utilization,
        32–34
    co-creation and, 28–29
    competition and, 29
    See also Social networks
Social mobile cloud, 45–50
    benefits of, 47–48

business competition and,
49–50

change and, 1–4

connotation of term, 45

defined, 2, 8–9

drawbacks of, 48–49

as infrastructure, 18–20, 46
(*See also* Digital
transformation)

network architecture for,
45–47, 49

technology needed for, 45–47

Social networks

digital transformation of,
7–9

personal and business online
presence, 32–34

as step beyond social media,
24–28

utilizing, 30–32

Social production.
See Co-creation ecosystems

Social shopping, 30–32, 61–62

Software

cloud computing and, 45–47

digitization and, 68–69

Solitary games, 98–99

Sophisticated sensors

digitization trend and, 67

mobile technology as, 35–36,
41–42

workforce collaboration with,
110–111

Spending, of resources (SAFE
concept), 149–151

Stored value

employee-employer
relationship and, 108–109

gamification and, 94–95

See also MONEY 2.0

Success, crucial skills for,
136–137

Supply chain

communication with, 25, 27,
47

gamification and, 102

MONEY 2.0 and, 86, 91

secure social networks and,
34

smartphone influence on, 7,
19

Systems thinking, 141–148

adaptability and, 157

change and, 122

chunking for, 141–144

goals for, 143–144, 146, 148

intention and, 144–145

tools for, 145–146, 147–148

TCP-IP, 46

Technology

change to organizational
structure, 106

digitization, 65–69

embedded, 57

labor jobs eroded by, 107,
127–128

merging of (*See* Digital
transformation)

technological change, 53–54

Telephony, mobile, 36–37, 67

Television industry, social media
used by, 18

Texting, advantages of, 128–130

Time issues

of digital transformation,
16–17

perspective of, 135–136

smartphone use in idle time,
27

Traffic information, systems
    thinking and, 145–146,
    147–148
Transaction
    improving, 2
    transaction cost economics,
    56–58
    See also MONEY 2.0

Transformation (ADAPT
    concept), 53–58

Video, mobile, 41–42

Word Lens (translation
    program), 40, 47

x86 architecture, 45–46